They Were Called Home

Copyright 2025 Patti Giglio
All Rights Reserved

ISBN: 979-8-3485-1967-4

Notice: The information in the book is true and complete to the best of my knowledge. It is offered without guarantee on the part of the author. The author disclaims all liability in connection with the use of this book.

All rights reserved. No part of this book may be reproduced or transmitted in any form whatsoever without prior written permission from the author except in the case of brief quotations embodied in critical articles and reviews.

This book is dedicated to my friends and family that have supported me in all my crazy endeavors, especially my husband Steve, children Liesl and Karl and my mom. It is also dedicated to all of those who I have loved and that have been called Home.

Crime and Punishment

AND THEN THERE WAS ONE

In the evening hours of October 15, 1892, tragedy struck Seneca Falls. The wall on the northside of the water flume that fed the Gleason Knitting Mills, which was 10' high and 3' thick, was in desperate need of repairs. After the water was drained from the flume earlier in the day, Michael Mansell and four other men, including the mill superintendent Benjamin Davis, climbed down into the deep trench at about 6pm to make the necessary repairs.

The men began to dig a little of the dirt from the bottom of the wall with pickaxes so that the base could be reinforced with a concrete mix. Without warning the massive wall of stone and dirt collapsed and crushed the men, except for Davis, under tons of debris. It took the rescuers two hours to recover their bodies.

Michael Mansell's funeral was held on October 18, 1892, at St. Patrick's Church. He left behind a wife, Mary, and daughter, Mary "Minnie" Mansell. Four years later, Mrs. Mansell would be forced to face the world alone.

A few years after her father's death, Minnie took was employed at the Mynderse farm on Cayuga Street about a mile outside of the village. She was a faithful house servant, mainly working in the kitchen, to Edward and his wife. At the same time, a young farm hand named Thomas Pelkinton was also under their employment. In the March 16, 1892, edition of the Democrat and Chronicle in Rochester, NY, Thomas Pelkinton was "a brawny, thick set man, with bad habits as to drinking and evil company, and was about a year ago under arrest here charged with arson."

Pelkinton was sweet on Minnie, but she rejected all his advances. He would accompany her to church, work, and home, hoping that he could change her mind. Unfortunately for him, she showed no interest in the young man. Unable to endure any more rejection, a horrible event began to unfold on March 15, 1896.

According to the Star-Gazette, the night before Pelkinton "slept at the barn at the Stanton House. He woke up at about 6 o'clock in the morning and walked to the farm to begin his work in the stables.

About 8 o'clock he went into the kitchen where Miss Mansell was working, and whatever in his appearance frightened her will never be known. She gave a scream which brought Mrs. Mynderse, half dressed, from her bedroom upstairs.

"When Mrs. Mynderse entered the kitchen, she saw Pelkinton grasp Miss Mansell by the arm, take out a revolver and aim it at the girl's head.

"Mrs. Mynderse appealed to the desperate man to desist but he turned on her with an oath and told her to get out or he would give her the first dose. Mrs. Mynderse turned and ran out shouting."

Minnie began to struggle with her assailant and used her "woman's strength against the brute force of a demon lover with murder in his soul." She tried to escape through a door near the outhouse, but it was bolted shut. Near that door her glasses were found on the floor crushed and broken. Unable to out-maneuver Pelkinton, Minnie was shot first in the cheek, which left a flesh wound. The second shot was "just above the left eye, and the muzzle of the revolver had been held so near to her face that all about the little circular hole that produced her death the flesh was blackened and burned with gunpowder." Minnie was just 20 years old at the time she was murdered.

Mrs. Mynderse brought back Solomon Sisco to help disarm Thomas Pelkinton, but they arrived too late, the deed had been done. Sisco searched for the "madman." When he checked the barn, he found the body of Pelkinton, killed by a self-inflicted gunshot wound, with his faithful spaniel curled up beside his master. Thomas was 28 years old.

The body of Thomas Pelkinton was turned over to undertaker C.S. Sanderson. His half-sister and stepfather requested that he be laid beside his mother at the Catholic cemetery. The church objected to the request because murder and suicide was a sin that should not be rewarded with eternal rest in sacred ground. Instead, his remains were given to Abram Fitch, the county master of the poor. At 5 o'clock on the evening of Match 16th, as the daylight waned, a horse and sleigh carried a simple casket down Fall Street. With just the undertaker and driver as witnesses, Pelkinton was quietly buried.

Mary "Minnie" Mansell's funeral was held on March 17th.

For days after the tragic event, the Mynderse farm became a tourist attraction. Curiosity drew people from around the countryside, in deep winter snow, to see where the murder had taken place.

There was no rest or peace for Pelkinton, Minnie or the Mynderse after the events on the Ides of March.

BIG MOOSE LAKE MURDER

Grace Mae Brown was born on March 20, 1886 in South Otselic, NY and left this earthly realm on July 11, 1906 at Big Moose in the Adirondacks.
Mysterious Death of Girl on Big Moose
Body of Grace Brown Taken from Lake, and Her Companion Missing
She Worked in a Factory
Left There with Two Men, One of Whom is Supposed to Have Accompanied Her to Lake
Utica, NY, July 13 – Wednesday forenoon a young and respectable looking couple left the southbound train at Big Moose, in the Adirondacks, and going to the Glenmore Hotel, registered as Carl Grahm, of Albany and Grace Brown of Otselic. The man carried a small handbag, on the outside of which was strapped a tennis racket. They remained at the hotel about 5 minutes, and, after stating that they had just stopped over one train, Grahm and his companion went to the boat landing, procured a light wood boat and went out on the lake. They did not return, and yesterday morning the was found bottom side up near Camp Craig.

Immediate search was taken up, and later yesterday afternoon the body of the young woman was taken from the lake near where the boat was found. Those who saw the body say that there were several marks and abrasions on the heads, and, as there are no rocks in the lake at that point, suspicion was at once aroused that the girl had been murdered.

The dragging of the lake was continued till dark and was resumed again this morning, but Grahm's body was not discovered, though his hat was picked up on the shore of the lake.

There was nothing on the body of the young woman by which she may be identified, and the coroner who was summoned has directed that the body be conveyed to Frankfort.

Grace Brown is the daughter of a farmer residing near Otselic, in Chenango County. For the last three years she had been working in a skirt factory in Cortland and four weeks ago she went to her home to spend her vacation. Last Monday she started to return to Cortland and left De Reyter in company with a Mr. Root and a man who was not known. Her father says that he has heard of his daughter speak of Mr. Grahm, but that he does not know the man.

It was supposed by the girl's father that his daughter was at Cortland, but since being informed of her drowning yesterday he has established the fact *that she has not been at the factory where she had been working and was not at her boarding house on Wheeler Avenue. He has no idea of the identity of Grahm, but he is satisfied from the description which has been sent him on the body found that it is that of his daughter.*

The lake was not rough in the least and the bay where the body was found was as smooth as a mill pond. When leaving the dock Grahm appeared to be acquainted with the use of a boat and the man who rented the boat though he was an experienced oarsman.

Parties have been searching the locality and notice has been sent to all railroad stations to be on the watch for Grahm should he be alive and attempting to make his escape.

Coroner Coffin says that in his opinion the girl was murdered, and that he will not change his mind unless the body of the man who accompanied her is discovered.

The Brooklyn Daily Eagle, July 13, 1906

The Post Standard (Syracuse), November 29, 1906

Grace was one of 9 children born to Frank and Betsy Brown. She graduated from a one-room school when she was 16. Grace worked as a farm hand in Norwich before being employed at the Gillette Skirt Factory. It is there that she met Chester and began what she thought was her Cinderella story began.

Chester Ellsworth Gillette's life was much different than Grace's. He came from wealth and power. He did missionary work with the Salvation Army and in China, after which he attended the divinity school at Oberlin College. Chester started at the very bottom in his uncle's factory and worked his way up the ranks to become the factory manager, and Grace's boss.

Whether Chester was truly in love with Grace, or he just used his power to take advantage of a naïve young woman, we may never know. Either way, they soon were involved in a very personal relationship, one that Chester wanted to keep secret. Things became complicated when Grace revealed to him that she was pregnant. He had weaseled his way into the upper crust of Cortland's society and if his secret relationship with Grace, and her pregnancy were discovered, he would no doubt be knocked down a few rungs on the social ladder.

Letters were found between Grace and Chester in which she begged him to accept responsibility for her current condition. Grace must have believed that her prayers of him coming around were finally answered when Chester suggested that they take a trip to the Adirondacks. She excitedly packed for the trip, which she hoped included a wedding ceremony.

Chester had other plans. He made all the arrangements and reservations under an assumed name. Their "wedding trip" started with a night in Utica, after which they left the hotel without paying. The couple spent the next night in Tupper Lake and then took a train to Big Moose, where the trip would end for Grace.

Chester rented a boat and rowed them out onto the lake. We can only imagine that Grace was on cloud 9, waiting for her life to change. She had no idea at that moment how right, and how wrong, she was. Chester rowed the boat to a secluded bay and bashed her head with the tennis racket. He then pushed her body overboard and upset the boat to make it look like an accident.

Chester was found 9 ½ miles away in Inlet and was arrested for the murder of Grace Brown.

The murder trial lasted just 3 weeks, November 12 to December 4, 1906, and it was a media sensation all over the world. The prosecution argued that Chester took Grace on the trip with the intention of murdering her...premeditated murder. Chester and his defense team had a different account of the event, or should I say several accounts. The defense first claimed that Grace had slipped in the boat, hitting her head as she fell, which caused the cut she had. Then their story changed to her being despondent and committed suicide. Chester even went as far as to say that they were never in a relationship at all. However, several love letters that Grace had written to him were entered into evidence. The jury heard all that they needed to and found Chester Ellsworth Gillette guilty of first-degree murder and sentenced him to death.

Chester was sent to prison at Auburn to await his sentence to be carried out. While there, he kept a diary. The last passage ended with "P.S. If it isn't any extra expense or too much trouble, please have 'Taps' played at the last...'Gone to be with Jesus.'"

On March 30, 1908, as Chester was strapped into the electric chair, he spoke these last words, "Tell my mother I am prepared to meet my God." At 6:14am, the switch was pulled, and 1800 volts of electricity coursed through his body. He lurched in the chair and his body shuddered for a minute before the warden ordered the power cut. At 6:18am, at the age of 24 years, Chester Ellsworth Gillette paid for his crime.

BROTHERLY LOVE

Cornelius and Patrick O'Brien of Newark, Wayne County were brothers who had a very turbulent and violent relationship that would survive two murder attempts, but not a third. Her sons' hatred of each other took a horrible toll on their mother Catherine. Though I am sure the rivalry was from birth, the first time a life was nearly taken was on September 11, 1895.

Cornelius was drunk when he came home that evening. He asked Catherine for some cider, to which she replied that it appeared that he had enough already. She went on to prepare dinner and Cornelius walked out of the room. He saw his brother Patrick and the two started to joke around until Cornelius said something that made Patrick mad. Patrick grabbed an axe and threw Cornelius to the ground with the intent of striking him in the head with it, which he did at least once. Cornelius took hold of the axe handle which broke. Enraged that his brother tried to kill him, combined with being intoxicated, he attacked Patrick with the broken axe handle. Patrick received sixteen large gashes on his head and four broken ribs.

Catherine begged Cornelius to stop the brutal beating and threw him out of the house. Patrick was in such bad shape that it was unknown if he would live or die. The doctor was called, which also meant the police showed up. A crowd began to gather outside the Newark home which was more than Catherine could handle. She grabbed a gun and threatened to shoot if they did not disperse.

The week only got worse for the O'Brien family. the next day the father, Patrick O'Brien was removed from the home by police officers and taken to the Wayne County Home as an insane invalid. A week later on September 18, 1895, he passed away.

On September 13th, Catherine was so distraught over her husband being taken away, Patrick mortally wounded at the hand of her own son and Cornelius on the run, that in a moment of insanity, she laid on the Central-Hudson Railroad tracks shortly before the express train was due to arrive. She refused to move, so the officers had to physically pick her up from the tracks. Due to her mental state, they took Catherine to the Wayne County Home until she regained her senses.

The second attempt didn't come to light until May 28, 1898, when Patrick was arrested for Cornelius's murder. Catherine had not slept for days and wandered around their make-shift home she shared with her sons Patrick, Cornelius and John, mumbling mostly to herself rather than to others – "My Con, my poor Con. Oh God, give me back my Con." After the death of her husband, the house was destroyed by a fire and what little insurance they had paid the balance on the mortgage, with no extra to rebuild. The family had been living in the barn for the last couple of years.

A reporter who visited the O'Brien home asked Catherine if the quarrel between Patrick and Cornelius in 1895 had anything to do with this recent incident. She replied that "they had apparently put aside all malice and hatred growing out of that dispute." Maybe that dispute, but not all the years of hatred.

What caused one brother to kill the other? Patrick gave a brief statement about the incident that appeared in the May 31, 1898 edition of the Rochester Democrat and Chronicle. "*Con and I were in the house together. John was outdoors. We had been having lunch, and we were singing when Con began talking about the war. He said that the Spanish soldiers and sailors were far superior to our men, and I did not agree with him. We had a few words, and soon I could see that Con was losing his temper. He continued to talk on the subject, and I contradicted one of his statements again. He then called me most hard named, and, with an oath, sprang up and seizing a pitchfork, which was standing close by, rushed me. I dodged, and picked up a hog stretcher such as is used in butchering. I warned him to keep off or he would get hurt. He made a thrust at me with the fork, and I struck back at him with the stretcher. I must have hit him, for he stopped for a minute, but came at me again. This time I struck him in the heart. I had to do it or he would have killed me.*"

According to Patrick, Cornelius had always hated him. Case in point an altercation that happened in 1897, as told during the coroner's inquest. Cornelius had apparently, in a drunken state, called their mother a liar. In Patrick's own words – "*He called her a liar, and I spoke and said she did not lie. He rushed out of the house, and picked up the axe, which was lying close by, and struck me over the head with it. I was not to blame, neither was I to blame for this last fuss. He has always hated me."* Oh, how easy it is to put all the blame for this "fuss" on the dead because dead men can't speak.

Neither John nor Catherine would say anything in their sworn testimony to incriminate Patrick. Catherine's testimony appeared that "she had been carefully coached" to make it "appear in the interest of the defendant." One son, and brother, was dead and they were trying to save another.

Finding the murder weapon was a monumental task, which Patrick made more difficult for them. In three separate statements, he gave three different versions of how Cornelius had died. First, he had used a hog stretcher, then it was an old potato knife, and in his final statement there was no knife just his fists. Several searches of the barn were made before the weapon was discovered; someone had hidden it well. The knife was on a small ledge above the stable's double door, completely out of sight. It had been recently washed but not well enough to get rid of the blood that had gotten inside the crevices of the handle.

After all the witnesses had been heard, the coroner's inquest jury deliberated for only a few minutes before indicting Patrick O'Brien for the death of Cornelius. "A knife wound inflicted by the hand of his brother, Patrick O'Brien, which knife was the immediate cause of his death."

On October 21, 1898 a grand jury found that Patrick O'Brien acted in self-defense when he killed his brother, Cornelius during a heated argument.

ISAAC WOOD

At 3 o'clock this afternoon, Isaac L. Wood, convicted of the murder of his sister-in-law, Rhoda Wood, by poisoning, at Dansville, this county, was executed. The execution took place in the enclosure attached to the jail.

A guard, composed of a company from Dansville and one from this village was present, and about five hundred spectators were about the premises. The execution was witnessed by about sixty persons.

The prisoner was brought in, attended by the deputy sheriff and a cleric. He addressed those present, protesting his innocence, and charging his conviction to prejudice and persecution. He said he died in the hope of a blessed immortality. At the conclusion of his remarks, he appeared to be in considerable agony. The sentence was then read, the drop fell, and Isaac L. Wood was "launched into eternity."

His remains will be taken to Avon until his friends take charge of them. He continued his protestations of innocence up to the latest moment of his existence.

The New York Times
July 9, 1858

What evil deed did Isaac Wood commit for him to deserve his premature demise? He was a cold and prolific killer, preying on those who cared for and loved him.

Isaac Wood was born on August 10, 1821, in New Providence, New Jersey to Daniel and Nancy Wood. There was a 15-year gap between Isaac and his brother David. When David left home in 1828, Isaac was left to run the family farm. This is where their stories are separated until 1854. While Isaac worked on the farm, David made his mark in Burns, NY and then in Dansville where in 1842 he started a successful shoe and leather business. It is in Dansville that David started a family with his wife Rhoda.

After 33 years on the farm, Isaac decided that didn't want to be a "tiller of the soil" like his father and set out to make his fortune in

Western New York like his older brother. He moved in with his brother and started a career as a produce broker, specializing in butter and eggs. David had a fine home with some land and had amassed an estate valued at close to $30,000 (more than $1 million in 2024). Instead of being happy for his brother's success; jealousy, temptation and greed crept into him.

In May 1855, while Rhoda and the children were on a trip to New Jersey, David became violently ill. The family was sent for, but he died before they could say their goodbyes. Within three weeks of David's death, Rhoda and the children became mysteriously sick with the same symptoms and Rhoda quickly died. Even though the doctors believed that the family had ingested a poisonous substance, the thought that it was murder was quickly dismissed. It was simply deemed as a tragic accident that left 2 children orphans and soon to be discovered...with no means of support. Where did the money go?

After his brother's death, Isaac gave a note to a produce firm in New York City for $2650 that he claimed was written by David. It was quickly determined to be a forgery. The suspicion that there was foul play in David and Rhoda's death began to grow. The suspicion only got deeper when Jospeh Welch, who had been living at the Wood home in 1857, found something very telling in the barn. Hidden in the loft was a package with three small packets containing a white powder, which was sent for chemical analysis. The results showed that each packet contained arsenic. This led to the exhumation of David and Rhoda's bodies, the contents of their stomachs also tested positive for arsenic. After a coroner's inquest, the jury concluded that Rhoda Wood's death came at the hands of her brother-in-law Isaac. Though it is not clear why he wasn't pinned for David's demise as well. A warrant for his arrest was drawn up, but Isaac was nowhere to be found.

After Rhoda's death, Isaac gained custody of the children whom he had tried to murder. He sent for his wife Sarah and his own child to join him in Dansville to live in his brother's house. When suspicions first started to turn on him, they quickly moved back to New Jersey without his niece and nephew...leaving them penniless orphans. Shortly after their return, Sarah and the child became mysteriously ill and died soon after, just like David and Rhoda. An analysis of their stomach contents returned the same results. With no witnesses and the loose ends tied, Isaac fled the area.

He turned up in Rantoul, Illinois where he worked as a farm hand. The Livingston County sheriff tracked him down and brought him back to Dansville to stand trial. The first trial in February 1858 ended in a mistrial, 8-4 in favor of guilt. The second trial started May 3, 1858, and within 2 ½ hours the jury came to an unanimous guilty verdict. May 17th, he was handed a death sentence to be carried out on July 9, 1858.

Isaac Woods' last words came at three different moments of his last day on earth. First, as he was taken to the gallows. "*Here I am, condemned by the laws of my country to die, in a few moments to end my life. And I shall pass away into another world. This world may look upon me as it pleases; but blessed be God, this is not my abiding place.*" The sheriff read the sentence and Isaac spoke again. "*Take this body; it nothing but a lump of clay. God knows that I am innocent, but you can't know it. It is between myself and God. In three minutes, I shall be free from my persecutors. I bid you all farewell forever. Blessed be God, I can die anywhere and at anytime.*" His hands were tied behind his back with a silk handkerchief. And moments before the door sprung below his feet, he spoke his last. "*Oh, Jesus, receive my spirit. Let me die as easy as you can.*"

Within half an hour after his body fell through the trap door and his neck was broken, the doctors declared him dead. The first execution in Livingston County was carried out.

And a funeral dirge played.

LAST TO SEE THE HANGMAN'S NOOSE

Roxalana and William Druse lived in Warren, NY and had a very tumultuous marriage. He had a reputation among his neighbors for having a bad temper, abusing his wife and incurring debt that he could not repay. Roxalana was unhappy with her lot in life and reportedly said at one time *"My advice is never to get married. I think it is a poor plan...It is a dreadful step to take, and it ought to have more consideration than people give it."*

On the morning of December 18, 1884, the couple, as usual, argued. But this time Roxalana had had enough. Was the action she took next the best option (shrugging my shoulders), unless we were in her shoes after 20 years of abuse, I cannot comment. Their daughter Mary tied a rope around William's neck and Roxalana shot him in the neck. (Though it does sound a little premeditated to me.) Frank, William's nephew, was forced to shoot his uncle as well. Roxalana proceeded to decapitate William with an axe, dismember him and burn the pieces of his body in the wood stove. She then threw his ashes, the axe and revolver into a pond.

It was a month before the neighbors realized that they had not seen William in a while. Roxalana tried to explain away his absence by telling everyone he was in New York City visiting family. But he unusual demeanor caused suspicions to be raised, and the police conducted an investigation into his disappearance. When Frank was questioned on January 16, 1885, he confessed to his role in William's murder and made certain he implicated Mary and Roxalana in the crime as well. It took just a quick search to turn up enough evidence to convict all three of them. Parts of William's charred body and the murder weapons were found in and by the pond. The most damning evidence though was the bloodstained floorboard in the Druse kitchen.

Roxalana's trial lasted just 2 weeks in October 1885 and ended in a guilty verdict handed down by an all-male jury and a sentence to hang by the neck until dead. The governor of New York received letters from angry men who offered to pay $10 to personally execute her, while others volunteered to buy the rope used to hang her.

After several attempts at appeals and a stay of execution, all denied, Roxalana Druse was hanged on February 28, 1887. When the lever was pulled and she fell through the trap door, her neck failed to break, and it took 15 minutes for Roxalana to slowly strangle to death. Many believed that she deserved the slow and painful death. The botched execution only solidified the need to use another form of execution in New York State and from then on, all death sentences were carried out in the electric chair.

LITTLE BETSEY BEATEN

"I want to tell you something, and can't, I'm ruined. I will tell you; I have whipped it to death, and if you will go and cure it, and keep it a secret, I will give you half of my property, even all."

This is the plea Stephen Arnold cried to Dr. Gaines Smith on January 12, 1805. "It" was Arnold's 6-year-old niece Betsey that he had severely beaten days earlier.

Arnold was described in 1805 as - *about 34 years of age, sandy hair, a little bald, speaks through his nose, has something of a down look, shews his upper teeth when speaking and is very abstemious to strong drink.* On the day of the incident, Arnold, a teacher in Burlington, was already in a foul mood after having dealt with students who refused to behave, and his frustration was soon taken out on Betsey. When he tried to give her a reading lesson, Betsey had trouble pronouncing the word "gig." Each time she said it wrong Arnold's anger grew. He believed that she was doing it on purpose and resolved to beat the stubbornness out of her - 6 times. When he took her outside the 6th, he lost complete control and brutally whipped Betsey for half an hour straight. After that she finally pronounced the word correctly, but the physical damage to her was irreversible. Betsey went to bed delirious with fever and spent the next days in and out of consciousness.

When Dr. Smith was called to the Arnold home, he was met by a very stern and inhospitable Susannah Arnold, who had the child on her lap. The doctor examined Betsey as best he could and gave Mrs. Arnold some advice on how to treat the child. At the time of the visit, he knew that Betsey was very sick, but Susannah told him not to return. The following day Stephen Arnold called for Dr. Smith again, but he suggested that Arnold call on two other doctors for help.

Stephen Arnold fled before Betsey took her last breath, he headed for the woods of western Pennsylvania. Otsego County offered a $200 reward for his capture. A man named Thomas

Cahoon from Chenango County sought to collect the reward and tracked Arnold to a saloon in Pittsburgh, Pa. Arnold knew he had been caught but rather than be taken alive, he threatened to shoot himself in the head. Cahoon batted to gun away before the trigger could be pulled and Arnold was taken to the local constable before he was transported back to Cooperstown for trial.

There is a very detailed transcript of the trial on record, which was almost unheard of in the still wild frontier of 1806. The transcript begins with *"Stephen Arnold, late of the town of Burlington, in the county of Otsego, farmer, not having fear of God before his eyes, but being moved and seduced by the instigation of the devil..."*

Arnold did not deny the charges, in fact gave a full confession of his deed. He admitted to whipping Betsey with 8 beech switches that he had trimmed and burnished in the fire. He recounted that he took her out 6 times and whipped her because the little 6-year-old would not properly say the word "gig." She was whipped on the calves of her legs and in the middle of her back, some of the bruises were so severe that they had turned black and sunk into her skin. Arnold was very candid that he and his wife had punished the girl before for various reasons.

When the doctors that examined Betsey took the stand, they determined that the beating given to her was so severe that even if immediate medical care was given, she would likely not have survived the wounds.

Besides the doctors only 3 others testified at the trial. One witness was Sally Adams, a girl that lived with the Arnolds. Sally said that Mr. Arnold had taken Betsey out 6 or 7 times to beat her and that the little girl was severely bruised, but the wounds did not really bleed. According to Sally, Stephen Arnold wept after he whipped Betsey and saw the damage he had inflicted on her tiny body.

Throughout the trial it was clear that Mrs. Arnold kept refusing to allow the doctors to treat the child and it seemed that she was a cold woman with no compassion for the suffering of little Betsey. But Stephen, on the other hand, was very remorseful according to all witness accounts. A neighbor had said that when they called on the Arnolds on January 12th, Mrs. Arnold did not want them to see Betsey, but before they left, they saw Mr. Arnold come to the girl's bedside and say *"Betsey, I have been a cruel creature, I had rather die myself than let you die."*

The prosecution's message to the jury was that the treatment of a child like this should not be allowed by law and should be punished to the fullest. And even though witnesses testified that Arnold was remorseful for his actions, his defense rested on the fact that Betsey's death was an accident and completely avoidable if she had just pronounced the word correctly. They squarely put Betsey's death on her own shoulders instead of where it belonged – on Stephen Arnold and even his wife Susannah, who would escape with her life.

It only took the jury 2 hours to deliberate and find Stephen Arnold guilty of the murder of Betsey. When the judge addressed Arnold, he stated that there was no other way that the jury could have gone. *"He was found guilty of whipping a young child of six years old, till she died, because she did not pronounce the word gig or jig, as he thought proper – he whipped her seven times, and was an hour and an half employed in the horrid transaction."* He also said, *"He supposed that a man of his age had obtained a tolerable education, having been a schoolmaster; and having the care of children, he ought surely to have known how to treat them."* The judge basically then said that the court could not and would not offer any mercy to that man based on the brutality of the crime.

Stephen Arnold was sentenced to death with these words, *"You are to be taken from hence to the place of confinement and from thence to the place of execution, and there to be hanged by the neck until you are DEAD! And the Lord have mercy on your soul."*

His date of execution was set for July 19, 1806 between 10am and 4pm. Around noon, a parade began with the participants in this order: the sheriff on horseback, clergymen, distinguished county and town gentlemen, a band that played a series of funeral dirges, a wagon with Stephen Arnold chained and seated on his coffin, and finally 2 companies of state militia armed with muskets and bayonets. Unfortunately, Stephen Arnold died from a heart attack on the gallows moments before the hanging was to take place. According to a witness of the execution, *"Wild excitement followed. Arnold fell as if he had been shot through the heart. Women shrieked; some of them wept aloud; some fainted; men raged and swore. The criminal was so detested for his cruelty that his escape from execution provoked a storm of fury. So indignant were the people that some rough fellows captured a dog, named him 'Arnold' and hung him on the gallows which had failed to do justice to his namesake."*

LOVE THY NEIGHBOR

During the early morning hours of March 21, 1915, Charles Phelps, a 90-year-old farmer, and his housekeeper Margaret Wolcott were shot and murdered in Phelps' house in West Shelby, Orleans County with a .22 caliber revolver. Though the sequence of events is mere speculation, the police did their best to piece together a timeline. At 11:30pm the killers knocked on Phelps' door and he set a lit lamp on the kitchen table before he answered it. When he started to open the door, a bullet passed into his chest. Phelps did not die that night, but the following day at the hospital in Medina. The sound of gunfire woke Margaret up. She rushed into the kitchen, saw the grisly scene and ran out the partially opened door. As she fled, a bullet pierced through the glass in the door before hitting Margaret under the left arm. She made it across the street to Charles Steilow's front door before she collapsed and died. Robbery was the motive. Money that Phelps had just withdrawn from the bank was missing and the contents of his dresser drawers were strewn about.

Articles in the newspaper told of how Charles Steilow found Margaret's lifeless body hours later. He then ran to Phelps' house and found Charles unconscious after which he summoned Dr. Erickson who lived nearby. The authorities began their investigation by interviewing the neighbors hoping to find a witness. Steilow and his cousin Nelson Green told the police that they heard nothing on the night of the murders and were both asleep. But at the coroner's inquest they testified that they heard cries from the Phelps house, looked out the window, saw nothing and went back to bed. Besides the inconsistency with their testimonies, Steilow and Green gave them three more reasons to suspect them. First...a week before the murders, Steilow was hired by Phelps as a farm hand. Second...Stielow and Green lived in a tenant house across the street that was owned by Phelps. And third...police discovered that Steilow owned a .22 caliber revolver, the same type of weapon sed in the crime. They were quickly arrested.

On April 21, 1915, Steilow "wrote" a long statement denying any involvement in the murders, but two days later he recanted the statement and confessed to being involved in the murders, but not to pulling the trigger. The two men's accounts could not have been more jumbled. Nelson Green always maintained that he was involved in the murders but was adamant that Steilow handled the gun. Just as Green did, Steilow pointed the finger at his cousin as the trigger man. With such a confused and jumbled mess of statements and recantations, were they guilty of the crime? Time would only tell.

Now the only thing that connected the men to the crime was a .22 caliber revolver, though there was no evidence that it was the actual weapon used. Dr. Albert Hamilton was the medical "expert," and he examined the bullets and gun but never test fired it. From his examination he determined that no other gun could have been the murder weapon. After the trial it was revealed that Hamilton had a fake medical degree. This alone should have been grounds for the dismissal of the case. But the jury agreed with the "good doctor" and on July 23, 1915, convicted Steilow and Green of 1st degree murder. Steilow was sentenced to death and sent to Sing Sing Prison to await his execution in the electric chair.

While in prison, Steilow's warden and supporters learned that he was mentally handicapped and could not read or write. The statement he agreed to, which turned out to be a confession to the murders, contained words and phrases that he would not have been able to understand.

His August 8, 1916 execution was rescheduled to July 14, 1916 and then again for July 29, 1916. Five hours before his execution was to take place, Justice Charles Guy ordered a stay of execution and offered him a new trial. The pre-trial hearing was set for August 22, 1916 in Rochester.

Before the hearing a former neighbor named Erwin King, a junk dealer who lived next door to Phelps at the time of his death and Clarence O'Connell were arrested, and they confessed to the murders of Charles Phelps and Margaret Wolcott. Even with the new evidence and the confessions, Steilow was denied a new trial by a different judge and was sentenced again to the electric chair.

Thomas O'Grady, a Buffalo detective, took an interest in the case and started a new investigation which resulted in the trial and conviction of King and O'Connell. On April 16, 1918, almost three years to the day after their trial, Steilow and Green were released from prison. Eight months later they were issued full pardons and had their citizenship restored. This trial is well discussed in law books today and is by some credited for the birth of modern forensic science.

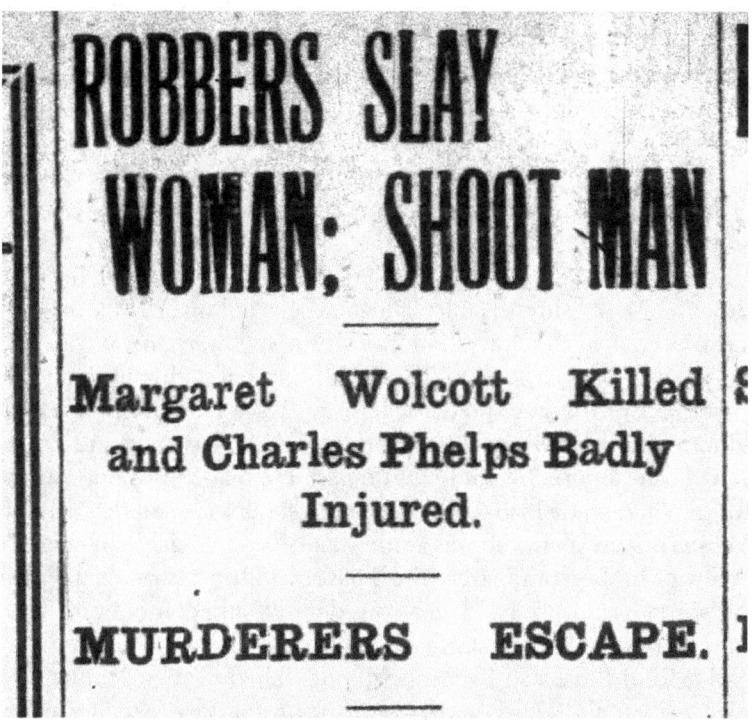

Buffalo Commercial March 22, 1915

MAKE MURDER NOT LOVE

John Love was a veteran of the War of 1812, who served on the celebrated frigate *USS Constitution*. On a side note, here are a couple of fun facts about the *USS Constitution*. The ship launched from the Edmund Hartt shipyard in the Boston, Massachusetts harbor in 1797, but after two centuries it still sails today. The US Navy has a 500,000-acre forest if white oaks, aptly named "Constitution Grove," to be solely used to repair the 227-year-old ship.

After his discharge, Love settled in Boston, NY and he was described as a "shrewd, calculating and clever" man. Even though Love served in the Navy honorably, war was war, and it was not unheard of or completely forbidden for an enlisted man to take a small part of the war spoils for himself. Love had amassed a tidy fortune that was believed to be from the *HMS Guerriere* and *HMS Java*, both captured by the *Constitution*. He made his money work for him and made loans with hefty interest rates to men throughout Western New York, he was somewhat of a "colonial loan shark." A few of his borrowers were the Thayer brothers; Isaac, Israel and Nelson, whom Love had lent a considerable sum of money to. The men were not too quick to make their payments and by December 1824, John Love had had enough and called in their loan. Love paid a visit to the Thayer farm where the brothers were getting ready to butcher the hogs. They gave him a warm welcome and asked him to wait in the house until they finished the butchering, after which they said they would discuss business. For being a navy veteran, Love was very gullible. The Thayers had no intention of paying him back. One brother shot him in the back of the head through the window. Then another charged into the house and attacked him with an axe. They dragged Love's body out of the house and buried him in a shallow grave, so shallow that the toes of his boots were sticking out of the ground.

The Thayers would have gotten away with the perfect crime, people disappeared all the time in the wilderness during the early

19th century. "Would have gotten away" are the key words though. After the murder, Israel Thayer was seen riding Love's horse. And the brothers were not the only people Love had loaned money. The neighbors became suspicious when they learned that Isaac had the promissory notes that belonged to Love and was trying to collect on those debts. When approached about why they had his horse and papers, the brothers came up with the story that John Love had admitted to them that he had killed a man in Pennsylvania and intended to flee to Canada before he could be arrested. The notes were supposedly given to Isaac as payment to keep his secret. No one believed the story that they had concocted and the search for Love was on. A $10 reward was offered to anyone who found his remains. People searched high and low until his body was finally found in Isaac Thayer's backyard.

All three of the brothers were arrested and tried for the murder of John Love. Within a matter of minutes, the jury came back with a guilty verdict, and they were sentenced to death. On July 17, 1825, in Lafayette Square in Buffalo; Isaac, Israel and Nelson Thayer were hanged before a crowd of more than 1,000 people. It was New York State's first triple execution.

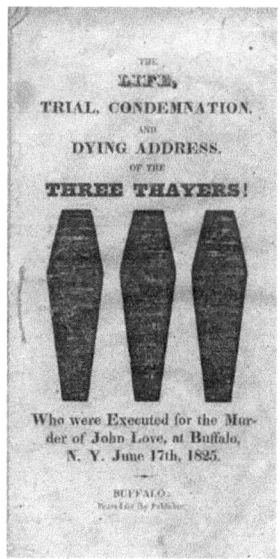

Three Thayers Trial Pamphlet

The pamphlet "The Mournful and Pathetic Ballad of the Murder of John Love" written by an anonymous author in 1825 that details the last little bit of is life –

On the fifteenth evening of last December
  in eighteen hundred and twenty four
tha invited Love to go home with them
  and tha killed and murdered him on the floor
first Isaac with his gun he shot him
  he left his gun and went away
then Nelson with his ax chopt him
  tell he had no life that could perceive

after tha had killed and mostly mortly bras's him
  tha drawd him out where tha killed thare hogs
tha then carried him of a pease from the house
  and deposited him down by a long

RESIGNED TO THE GUN

1814 was a rough winter for those stationed at the Fort Hill encampment near Buffalo, epidemics and starvation ran rampant. Hundreds died, both military and civilians as many of the 400 residents that were left homeless when the British burned the village of Buffalo to the ground on December 31, 1813 were housed there. John Black, Mahlon Christie, Isaac Kent and George Orcote were caught deserting the camp and their duties. That dereliction of duty came with a high price...execution by firing squad. In a letter home, a soldier wrote *"Four for desertion and one for mutiny have lately been shot at the camp, which nearly caused a rebellion."*

Jarvis Hanks, a War of 1812 soldier and witness to the executions, gives the most detailed narration of the events. It is so detailed and absorbing that it would not be fair to paraphrase it, so here it is in its entirety.

"Five men were sentenced to be publicly shot for the offense of desertion. They were dressed in white robes with white caps upon their heads, and a red target fashioned over the heart. The army was drawn up into a hollow square to witness the example that was about to be made of their comrades who had proved recreant to the regulation of the service.

Five graves were dug in a row, five coffins placed near them, also in a line, with distance between the coffins and graves to enable the criminals to kneel between them. About twelve men were assigned to the execution on each offender. Their guns were loaded by officers, and they were not permitted to examine them afterwards until they had fired.

All things being in readiness, the chaplain made a prayer, the caps were pulled down over the eyes of the poor culprits, and the word of the command given: 'Ready! Aim! Fire!' They all fell! Some into their graves, some over their coffins.

At this time one of the condemned slowly arose from his recumbent position to his knees and was assisted to his feet. His first remark was, 'By God, I thought I was dead.' In consequence of his youth and the peculiar circumstances of his case, he has been reprieved, but the fact was not communicated to him until this moment...The platoon assigned to him had guns given to them which were not charged or at least had nothing but powder in them." Can you imagine?

STREAMS OF DEATH

There are two Murder/Murderer Creeks in New York State, and both have a history steeped in death and waters that ran red with blood.

In the late eighteenth century, a family by the name of Stacy lived along the banks of Moodna Creek where it emptied into the Hudson River. Relations between the settlers and Natives were strained, but the Stacys had forged a friendship with an old Indian named Naoman. He broke bread with the family at their table and plated with their two young children. Even though they were friends, they still had not gained Naoman's trust. It would finally be won but at a tragic cost.

Naoman visited the log home and sat at the table with Mrs. Stacy several days in a row with a heavy burden on his mind, unsure if she could keep the secret he needed to tell. Finally, she asked flat out if he had something on his mind, to which he replied – "It will cost me my life if it is known, and the white-faced women are not good at keeping secrets." She assured the old man that even in the face of certain death she would tell only her husband.

He told her how the people of his tribe had grown weary of the settlers encroaching on their lands. And that when night fell on that day, they intended to attack and massacre all those who took what was theirs. Naoman told her to gather the children and her husband, to leave secretly but swiftly. He warned her to "be quick and do nothing that may excite suspicion."

Mrs. Stacy wasted no time finding her husband, who had been fishing at the river. After she relayed to him what Naoman had told her, they planned an escape. A few belongings were collected before the family headed for their boat which they found filled with water. Precious time ticked away as they drained it.

The old man was worried that the actions of the Stacys would cause suspicion, but it was his comings and goings at their homestead over the previous months that had the family under surveillance. Though they tried to make their departure appear routine, the timing set off an alarm and a young warrior that watched over them ran to the Indian village to report the Stacys' movements. Unwilling to allow any settler to escape death, five braves took to canoes and hunted them down like dogs after a fox.

As they gained on them, Mr. Stacy raised his gun to fire, but his wife convinced him that to shoot would mean certain death if they were captured. He heeded her warning and continued to push down the creek to try to out-paddle their pursuers. But the Indians overtook them and dragged them ashore. Before taking the family to the village, the Stacys' home was set on fire.

Once at the village, the old men and Naoman gathered to interrogate the family. It was clear that there was a traitor among them and no matter what means necessary, they planned to get a name out of Mr. or Mrs. Stacy. Mr. Stacy refused to betray Naoman. They then worked on his wife, knowing that white woman had loose tongues. To persuade her cooperation, two men stood by her children ready to kill them when the order was given. Mrs. Stacy told a lie, that a vision came to her in a dream while she slept telling her to run away with her family. An old Indian did not believe her and said "the Great Spirit never designs to talk in dreams to a white face. Woman, thou hast two tongues, and two faces. Speak the truth, or thy children shall surely die." He would ask her three times the name of "the red man who betrayed his tribe," and each time she refused to answer. As the third question was answered with silent contempt, tomahawks were raised over the children's heads.

Naoman shouted for the men to stop. "White woman," he said "thou hast kept thy word with me to the last moment. I am the traitor. I have eaten of the salt, warmed myself at the fire, shared the kindness of these Christian white people, and it was I that told them of their danger. I am a withered, leafless, branchless tree. Cut me down, if you will; I am ready." With a blow from a tomahawk, he fell dead at Mrs. Stacy's feet. Naoman wanted to believe that by showing his fellow tribesmen the family's loyalty to a friend, it would save their lives. But his moving speech did not change their fate. Mr. and Mrs. Stacy, as well as their two young children, were struck down where they stood.

The death of the Stacy family was not the only murder that took place along the banks of Moodna Creek, which came about its nickname Murderers Creek honestly.

In August 1813, the small village of Athens, New York was rocked by the most shocking crime. After an evening out to visit her sister, Sally Hamilton left her company just about fifty yards from the front door of the house Sally shared with her parents. Sally disappeared and never made it to the door. For days her family and neighbors searched for her. Saturday afternoon, just three days after she was last seen, Sally's lifeless body was found in Moodna Creek just ¾ miles from her home. She was bruised from head to toe and one of her arms had been broken. The coroner was certain that due to how brutally she had been attacked, her death came at the hand of someone else. But who?

Four years after Sally Hamilton's murder, Thomas Lent confessed to killing her with the help of Johnathan Sickler. During his confession, the detail given by Lent gave the authorities no doubt that they were responsible for the demise of this young woman. However, at the trial, the testimony provided by Lent and Sickler was full of contradictions and absurdities. Too many questions came to light as to whether the men were present at the killing, and as a result they were acquitted.

There was yet one more murder associated with this Hudson River tributary. The headline of an August 21, 1935, newspaper read – "*Mother Happy After Killing Two-Year-Old Son in Creek.*" The mother's tale was that of heartbreak. Dorothy Sherwood was a dancer with a vaudeville troupe when she met and fell in love with her husband Fred, who ran the projector in a movie house. The two married and life was good. Little Dorothy was born, followed by Jimmie five years later.

Fred began to feel sick and couldn't work in the dark room of the movie house. The doctor's diagnosis was devastating, Fred's body was slowly being consumed by tuberculosis. They spent the little money that they had on medicine to treat it. After a hard-fought battle, Fred died six months before his wife's desperate crime. Little Dorothy went to live with Fred's family in Calicoon, but Jimmie stayed with his mother. While Dorothy got a job in a restaurant, she still struggled to care for her son. At the end of her rope, she did the unspeakable.

After her shift was over, Dorothy put little Jimmie into his baby carriage, bought him a chocolate bar with her last nickel and walked the four miles from Newburgh to Moodna Creek. She found a secluded spot along the bank and let her boy wade and play in the water for half an hour or so. Dorothy decided to join him and splash his face with the water, she listened to him giggling as she held him and then slowly held his head under water until he drowned. Dorothy flagged down a truck passing by for a ride back to Newburgh under the guise that her son was sick and in need of a doctor. Once she was in town, Dorothy walked into the police station to confess to the mercy killing of Jimmie. She was arrested and sentenced to death after a jury found her guilty of murder. After serving only a few years she was released.

Dorothy Sherwood and baby Jimmie

Nearly three hundred miles west is Murder Creek, outside of Buffalo in Akron, New York. The legend of it is from the early 1820s. It goes something like this.

John Dolph and Peter Van Deven were sent to build a sawmill along Murder Creek. One night John heard a woman's scream in the woods outside his cabin, as he opened the door to investigate an Indian girl rushed in begging for help. No sooner had Dolph closed the door, a man pounded on it and demanded that the girl be given to him. The man named Sanders pushed his way into the cabin looking for the girl. He told Dolph and his wife that she was a fugitive from Grand River, Canada and he was going to return her to the authorities. The reason for her arrest, which made no sense, was that she was in love with and wanted to marry a "bad Indian" and her father put her into Sanders' custody.

The was well-hidden and Sanders, though convinced she was near, angrily and reluctantly left. But he remained in the shadows to watch what Dolph would do next. The girl had been stowed in a cavern where she was safe and eventually had fallen asleep. When she awoke the story of her troubles was told.

Her name was Wild Rose, and her home was a mile below the Tonawanda Falls near Spirit Lake. Wild Rose's mother died years ago, and Sander's had murdered her father Great Fire. Before he killed her father, Sanders had tried for more than a year to get her to marry him. The request was repeatedly turned down because Wild Rose was in love with Gray Wolf, a Seneca brave. Not willing to be denied what he wanted, Sanders vowed to kill anyone who came between him and Wild Rose.

Great Fire and his daughter left under the cover of darkness to take her to safety at Cattaraugus, where Gray Wolf would meet her. After they walked for a while they stopped to rest. Unbeknownst to Wild Rose and her father, Sanders had been following them and he was close behind. He approached them and offered amends for his past discretions and even said he would accompany them to Cattaraugus and provide them with protection. As Wild Rose stood up, Sanders hit Great Fire with a club and killed him instantly. She ran from the scene and towards a light that she saw in the woods – the Dolph cabin.

It was believed that Sanders was on his way back to Buffalo. When word reached Gray Wolf, he rushed to the side of Wild Rose. Dolph and Van Deven buried Great Fire. As Gray Wild and Wild Rose chanted the death song at the grave of her father, Sanders jumped from the brush brandishing an axe. The odds were even when Gray Wolf grabbed his tomahawk. A struggle ensued and when their weapons were lost, hunting knives were drawn. Both men were bloody and wounded. Sanders fell dead first, and as Gray

Wolf, the victor, turned to Wild Rose he crumpled and died beside the grave of Great Fire. He was buried on that spot.

Wild Rose had no place to go, so she returned to Dolph's cabin and there she stayed. She spent hours at the graves of her father and her one true love. One day she was gone longer than usual, and the Dolphs searched for her. Wild Rose was found lifeless on top of Gray Wolf's grave, dead from a broken heart.

More than three quarters of a century, the bloody legacy of Murder Creek was justified. On October 31, 1890, Sarah McMillan lured Delia Brown, six years old, and Nellie May Connors, ten years old, to the bridge behind the Akron Cement Works. Fifty-two feet above the rocks and water, Sarah threw the girls over the side. Nellie hit the bridge abutment in the fall which crushed her skull and killed her instantly. Delia was not as lucky, she suffered from internal injuries and lingered in excruciating pain for hours until she was found. After throwing the little girls to what she hoped was to their deaths, Sarah jumped from Mechanic Street Bridge in an unsuccessful suicide attempt. She was rescued from the water by Simon Brown, the father of Delia. At the time he had no idea the deed she had just committed.

Sarah and Simon were not strangers. Sarah lived in the Brown home and was secretly in love with the older man. When Delia was found eight hours after the fall, she was conscious enough to point the finger toward her attacker. At the time no one knew why Sarah targeted the girls. At the coroner's inquest the truth would come out when a letter written to her aunt was read. It was a letter which would draw both sympathy and condemnation from the jurors.

Dear Aunt - When you get this letter, I will be far from earth. I am sick and tired of living, as I told you my last hope is come at last. I am thankful to die, people rebuke me for things that I am guilty of and as I have no one to love me I can go in peace. My heart I leave in Akron with the one I always spoke to you of as he seems to not care for me. I know it is a sin for me to put an end to myself, but I am not the only one. Now, if only I had my little brother with me, I would be happy. If I had died when I was young how thankful I would have been, but as it is I must die as it is. So, tell my sister that I lover her as much as ever, but would not stay with her. I hope you will see to them, as I know you will, and when I am dead. I will come to you and explain but do not fear me, I will not hurt you and the man I loved will know me as a frequent visitor. Oh dear, if it was only over how thankful I would be. I think I will take someone with me, so I will close my last letter on earth, hoping God will do justice, with me as He does with everybody. So, when you will find my body in the basin in Buffalo. Please bury me in Akron as I will be near my loved one. So, goodbye from Sadie, Your no more niece.

It appeared that the girls were the victims of a love triangle. Sarah was in love with Simon Brown, but he was keeping company with Nellie's mother. She felt that killed the girls would tear them apart. And though Sarah had placed to kill herself, she wanted to make sure that no one lived happily ever after.

At the trial Sarah McMillan was acquitted of Nellie May Connors' murder and the attempted murder of Delia Brown on the grounds of insanity. A diagnosis of epileptic insanity sent her to Buffalo State Psychiatric Center until August 1893. After her release, she disappeared without a trace.

These are the tales of two creeks with very bloody pasts that earned them the nickname of Murder.

THE BUFFALO HANGMAN

Patrick Morrissey was born on St. Patrick's Day 1844 and his parents named him after the patron saint of Ireland. Soon after the Morrissey family immigrated to America and settled in Buffalo. Whether by accident or illness, the Morrissey patriarch died not long after their arrival leaving his wife Ann to provide for Patrick and his 3 sisters. To make ends meet, she kept a boarding house in one of the poorest areas of Buffalo called the "infected district."

Patrick was not an easy child to say the least and Ann was a hard woman with a fiery temper, which drove a wedge between Ann and her son at times. When he was 21 years old, he was arrested for larceny and a jury sentenced him to 3 ½ years at Auburn. But 8 months later he was granted a pardon from the governor for the simple reason of getting Ann to stop pestering him. After his release he worked as a sailor. When on land he stayed at his mom's boarding house and spent most of his days drunk. On June 22, 1872, he went on a bender and then came home. The following morning, he went out to drink more. When he came home around 2pm, the people boarding at Ann's said he had a "wild look about him." He began to argue with is mother and she threatened to call the "watch," or police. This enraged him even more. With a carving knife in his hand, he grabbed Ann from behind, spun her around and stabbed her in the chest.

Patrick waited for the police to arrive. Still in a drunken state, he denied the crime, then confessed to it only to deny it again. At his trial only 2 weeks later, his attorney pled a defense of temporary insanity "caused by liquor and a disposition to light-headedness, resulting from a blow received on his head." At the conclusion of the 3-week trial, he was found guilty of murder and sentenced to hang at the Erie County Courthouse. Before 12 invited witnesses on September 6, 1872, Patrick dressed in a black robe fell through the trap door and had his neck snapped by the noose.

John Gaffney was arrested when he was 19 for theft, which would become a pattern throughout his 29 years on this earth. It is argued that Gaffney shot fellow thief Partick Fahey on May 7, 1872, at Ted Sweeney's saloon on Canal Street. Gaffney had accused Fahey of "causing trouble" to which Fahey proceeded to insult Gaffney. Gaffney, according to the only witness who came forward, then pulled out a revolver and shot Fahey 3 times. Seems like a senseless murder to me. Sticks and stones may break my bones, but names will never hurt me.

Gaffney tried to play the insanity card to save his life, but the jury saw right through it and found him guilty. He was sentenced to hang by the neck until dead. Before a crowd of about 100 witnesses on February 14, 1873, Gaffney stood on the scaffold and said these last words, "*I hope and pray to God that you will believe me and forgive me. I beg pardon for all the crime I have done, and I forgive all who have injured me.*" At 12:02pm the trap was released. Gaffney's neck broke within seconds, but his heart still beat for 22 minutes more.

Of all the hangings in Western New York in the 19th century, you may ask what makes these 2 executions special. Morrissey and Gaffney have the honor of being the only criminals executed by a future US president and executioner. Grover Cleveland was the Erie County sheriff at the time and then the mayor of Buffalo. He would later be elected the 22nd (1885) and 24th (1893) President of the United States.

Young Grover Cleveland, the Buffalo hangman

THE CRIME AND HANGING OF JAMES MCLEAN

In the spring of 1807, James McLean murdered two of his neighbors - William Orr and Archibald McLaughlin on Graney Road outside of Caledonia. A crime that began with a disagreement over a tree.

William Orr cut down a tree that McLean believed belonged to him. The funny thing was that none of the men owned any property, they had all been squatters on over 40,000 acres of land. McLaughlin saw McLean and Orr in a heated debate and tried to reach them before things escalated further. He was not able to intervene. McLean raised his ax and crashed it down on Orr's head. Orr was dead before he hit the ground. McLaughlin went to his knees beside his friend's body and McLean, still filled with mad rage, swung the ax once more striking Mc Laughlin in the heart. A young man named McColl wrestled the ax from McLean's hand before he could claim another victim.

McLean knew that the law would soon come to apprehend him, so he fled into the dense forest moving farther from Caledonia. After a week on the run, he grew hungry and tired. Thinking he had gone far enough to not be recognized and visited a tavern in Canandaigua. He was mistaken, the militia was tipped off and McLean arrested.

In front of a jury of his peers, McLean was tried and convicted of the death of William Orr. The jurors could not clearly decide how the events that lead to the death of McLaughlin played out - whether he was killed during the two men's scuffle or after. The sentence was heavy one, which made him the first man to be hanged in Genesee County.

It is best to let the account of the first public hanging in the county, which took place on August 28, 1807, be told by a witness. "*When the weight fell, the rope broke, and McLean fell to the ground. He soon recovered from the shock and rising to his feet, expressed a strong desire not to be hanged again.*" There was great debate as to what should happen next. Some believed that his sentence had been carried out, he was hanged and whether it was successful or not did not matter. Others had the opinion that even though he was convicted on just one death, he killed two men and he should be hanged twice.

Sheriff Benjamin Barlow was determined to see the execution be carried out. The crowd was not disappointed by the second attempt, death came quick once the weight dropped. The body of James McLean is said to lie in an anonymous grave at the Batavia Cemetery on Harvester Avenue.

THE SOUND OF THUNDER

Robert A. Douglas was hanged on August 29, 1825 on Gallows Hill before a crowd of ten thousand, though I believe that after 200 years of the legend being told, that number may have been exaggerated. His crime – the supposed cold-hearted murder of Samuel Ives.

When Douglas came to the area from Philadelphia in 1823, he did not exactly choose the best characters to associate with and fell into the wrong crowd. Or he them into the unsavory characters that they became. He befriended the Mayberry's who ran the tavern near Cameron Mills on the Canesteo River. It was rumored that peddlers would often go missing without a trace from the tavern. Like the Benders, aka the Bloody Benders, in the Kansas frontier half a century later. Douglas married one of the Mayberry daughters and became a willing participant in the family crime ring. When Thomas Mayberry's home was eventually searched, the authorities found a cache of stolen goods including watches, jewelry and money.

The death of Samuel Ives was the result of a crime connected to the syndicate. Douglas had been accused by Ives of theft and passing him a counterfeit bill. The events leading to Ives demise are still disputed to this day, however the end is not – Ives died within minutes after being stabbed and Douglas was on the run.

After Douglas stabbed Ives, he fled into the woods heading for the Alleghany Mountain foothills. The local militia were given orders to hunt the murderer down. All accounts say that after a few days on the run, he grew tired and hungry, . In a momentary lapse of judgment, Douglas snuck into the barn of James Hallet to steal some food, but instead he walked right into a trap.

Some versions of Ives death portrayed Douglas as a cold-blooded killer, while others shoed that Douglas acted purely in self-defense. The Crooked Lake Review published this version in the Spring 2000 edition.

"Douglas was traveling the area selling goods from a backpack, that many whispered had been stolen goods from another unlucky peddler. Some of his customers claimed to have received bogus bills from Douglas as their change. One such dissatisfied patron was Samuel Ives from Troupsburg. Ives vowed to get even with Douglas who had given him a phony dollar bill. Ives' revenge would have to wait since Douglas had been jailed on counterfeiting charges.

A neighbor to Douglas, James Hallet, paid Douglas' five-hundred-dollar bail. A few days later, Douglas was spotted by Ives as he passed the vengeful man's home. Ives raced after him, waving the five-dollar bill in his hand. Douglas denied the charge. Ives then grabbed Douglas, who broke free only to be caught again and knocked down by Ives. In his wrath, Ives began choking Douglas, who then pulled out a pocketknife. After being stabbed, Ives staggered to his house, fell on a bed and died."

A newspaper article in The Farmer's Cabinet from Amherst, New Hampshire on September 25, 1824, offered its readers a vague account of the event.

"...Robert Douglas, who had been in Bath jail for passing counterfeit money, and has been bailed out, was passing a Mr. Ives, to who he has passed the money, a fight ensued between them, when Douglas drew a dirk and stabbed Ives three times, so that he died in about ten minutes."

Douglas was tried twice for Ives death. The first was ruled a mistrial due to the misdeeds of a juror. Douglas was found guilty at the second and sentenced to hang by the neck until dead.

The hanging, which took place on April 29, 1825, supposedly drew thousands of spectators who packed picnic lunches. The first execution in Steuben County felt more like a country fair than a man's impending death. Vendors even sold gingerbread and cider.

Just before noon, Douglas was brought from the jail and was seated on his coffin in the back of a wagon. As the wagon began to move toward the gallows, a military band played Chopin's "Funeral March."

When asked if he had any final words, Douglas again professed his innocence, that he had meant no harm to Ives and that his death was only in self-defense. But the remarks fell on deaf ears; the jury had spoken, and the crowd was not gathered to hear the final pleas of a condemned man but to see a murderer hang. A black hood was placed over his head and the noose around his neck. A passage from *Stories of the Canisteo Valley* by William Stuart described the incredible scene that followed.

"*While people gaped, there came a pounding of hooves along the road that lead from Bath. A terrible figure advanced at a gallop. It was a horseman all dressed in black, with a black mask over his face, while his mount was also sable. As he reached the scaffold, he checked his steed, leaned over, pulled a rope and then thundered down the road and no man in all the crowd, save probably two or three, could say who he was. The drop fell and amid a great gasp from the crowd, Douglas was snatched into eternity.*"

Douglas did not die that easy of a death, his neck was not broken by the fall and he slowly strangled until all the life completely left his body.

The innocence or guilt of Douglas was debated at the time. Some believed they had witnessed an innocent man be executed. It was a belief that was strengthened when the sky drew dark, and a wicked electrical storm blew in the moment Douglas drew his last breath.

The legend of Robert Douglas lives on in the poem, *The Ballad of Robert Douglas* written by an anonymous hand.

THE TRUNK MURDER

Sarah Brennan took her last breath on April 23, 1908, in the home of her neighbor and tenant Mary Farmer. Her death was a plan six months in the making.

Mary, along with her husband James, lived in the old Barton Tavern in Brownville which was owned by the Brennans. But Mary had her eyes set on a prize greater than the broken-down home they occupied. Her diabolical plan was set into motion on Halloween 1907. She went into the law offices of Burns and Burns to make a real estate transaction. Under the guise of Sarah Brennan, she had the clerk file papers that put the deed of the Brennans' house, a much nicer abode, into the name of Mary Farmer. Word got around town that Sarah had sold Mary the property, a rumor that she vehemently denied. Mary bided her time until the perfect moment made itself known. They continued to pay the Brennans rent and the Brennans remained in their home.

April 23rd proved to be the opportunity that Mary had been waiting for. On the way to an appointment, Sarah paid her a visit. Though the reason for the call remains a mystery today, it proved to be a fatal decision. Home alone, Mary opened the front door, and Sarah was last seen entering it around 10 o'clock that morning.

Within a matter of hours, Mary began to move into the Brennan home, which she had just six months earlier had fraudulently deeded to herself. She told her husband James that Sarah confided in her that she planned to divorce Patrick, leave town, and sell her the property for mere pennies on the dollar, money that Mary had borrowed from her family. For some reason James bought her story, no questions asked and quickly enlisted his brother's help with the move. As they moved all their belongings, a large heavy trunk tied with clothesline turned up, which Mary told James was a set of fine china. The real identity of the contents would soon be discovered.

When Mr. Brennan returned home from work, he was surprised to see the Farmers in his house and his wife nowhere to be found. After James told him that they were now the owners of the property, he began searching for Sarah. At the time, Patrick believed his wife to be alive. But a visit to Burns and Burns would point to foul play being responsible for her disappearance. Francis Burns described Mary Farmer as the woman who came to his office on October 31, 1907, not Sarah Brennan.

Patrick went to the authorities with his suspicions and immediately police investigators visited Mary and James Farmer to conduct a search of the house. No evidence of a crime was found until they reached one of the bedrooms where they discovered two trunks stacked upon each other. They took particular interest in bottom trunk, most likely because it was tied with a clothesline. Mary told them that the trunk belonged to James, but he quickly stated that that was a lie. Mary then told them that it only held clothes and boxes, to satisfy their curiosity, the investigators wanted to see for themselves. They were not prepared for what they were about to discover. The following account in the *Watertown Daily Times* detailed the discovery.

One of the officers lifted it and found it rather heavy. The rope was untied, but the trunk cover would not budge. It was locked and the Farmers averred that the key was lost, or at least that they could not find it at that time. Thereupon Sheriff Bellinger broke the lock with a hammer and opened the cover.

Odor of Decaying Flesh - The sickening odor of decaying flesh pervaded the room. At the first glance it seemed that the woman's statement had been true, for a black cloth covered the contents of the trunk, which was little more than two-thirds filled up. But when the cloth was pulled back a trifle the stocking outlines of a human foot and leg protruded. The cloth was the black skirt of a woman.

The body was resting upon the face, the legs bent at the knees and the feet sticking upwards nearly to the top of the trunk. One ed of the trunk was smeared with blood and here the horrified officers disclosed the head, blood-clotted, the back crushed in as with a blunt instrument. There was considerable blood in the bottom of the trunk and some of it had oozed through upon the floor in the corner.

Mr. and Mrs. Farmer disclaimed all knowledge of the body. They knew nothing about it, they said.

Finding an Axe - Among the first finds made by the officers was an axe in the backyard which was turned over to Coroner Pierce and will probably be submitted to Dr. Isabelle Meader for analysis. The axe was discolored, but whether from rust or blood could not be told. There was also some substance upon it that might be brains. Sheriff Bellinger found the axe.

First Mary told the police that she struck Sarah Brennan on the back of the head with an axe before stuffing her body into an empty trunk she had waiting. It was cold, premeditated murder. But she quickly changed her story and pinned the heinous act on James. She also denied the Halloween visit to Burns and Burns office. Both Mary and James Farmer were taken into custody for Sarah's murder. The conflicting stories and James' laissez-faire attitude about Sarah's disappearance did not help his case. However, Patrick Brennan did not believe he had been involved.

I don't believe Jim Farmer killed Sarah. I have known Jim all my life. We were boys together, went to school together and have been good friends always. When they opened the trunk before him and his wife, I turned to him and said, 'My God, Jim, can it be that you have done this?' Jim answered me: 'So help me, God, Patsy, if I was to die this minute, I don't know nothing about it.'

No, I cannot believe Jim Farmer killed my wife. But I do believe Mrs. Farmer did, and I want to see her get the electric chair for doing it. If Jim did have anything to do with it, I want him to pay the penalty, too.

Interestingly, on the morning that Sarah Brennan's body was found, the Farmers sent for a catholic priest to bless their "new" home. The Farmers were not religious at all, so this was an unusual request. The *Norwood News* reported this oddity in their May 19, 1908, edition.

Surely it was with no sincerity of purpose that on the morning of the day the mutilated body of Mrs. Brennan was found in the trunk, that the Farmers dispatched little George Farmer to the rectory with the request that the good Father come to the Brennan home. With characteristic willingness he hurried to the home on "Paddy Hill," thinking as he crossed the river that someone needed the sympathy or spiritual advice that he might give; that he had given to others in the little village of Brownville in hours of sorrow and suffering.

The Farmers had not attended Father Pontier's church regularly; had gone at remote intervals if at all. They were not sufficiently identified with the church as to carry to their neighbors the idea that they gave much thought to things spiritual. And yet, after Mrs.

Brennan had been murdered and placed in a trunk, and the trunk carried from the Farmer home to the Brennan home, they, in their utter depravity, and probably with the idea that a visit by Father Pontier would be observed by neighbors and have the effect of producing a favorable impression, sent for him to perform certain solemn rites in connection with their "new home." At the very hour when the sacred service was performed the Farmers, present and professing sincerity, had concealed in that rear room of the house the ghastly remains of their awful work, which was disclosed in the afternoon on that day by Sheriff Bellinger.

Mary Farmer

Mary Farmer would confess, then recant, confess again and recant again. At the end of April 1908, Mary made her fifth confession. A week later she began to act, and I emphasize ACT, as if she was insane. She was described, in a term from the time, as "putting up a bluff." Her performance did not work, as the coroner handed down his verdict on May 8, 1908, which was reported in the *Watertown Daily Times*.

Mrs. Sarah Brennan came to her death through blows inflicted by Mary Farmer at the latter's home in the village of Brownville on the morning of Thursday, April 23, is the verdict reached by Coroner Charles E. Pierce after a careful investigation of the case, which he has been conducting since the body of Mrs. Brennan was discovered in a trunk at the Brennan house on the afternoon of April 27.

The name of James D. Farmer, husband of Mary Farmer, is not mentioned in the decision. Coroner Pierce evidently leaving to the grand jury the question of whether or not the husband was an accomplice.

The coroner apparently concludes that Mrs. Brennan met her death almost immediately after entering the Farmer home on the fatal Thursday. That the deceased came to her death wounds on the head inflicted by one Mary Farmer, of the town of Housnfield, Jefferson County, NY, in a back middle room of what is known as the old Barton House, the home of the said Mrs. Farmer, situated on what is known as Paddy Hill in the town of Hounsfield, Jefferson County, NY, on April 23, 1908, between the hours of 8:30 and 9:30 in the forenoon.

That the said Sarah Brennan came to her death by said wounds produced by said Mary Farmer with a hammer, hatchet, or similar instrument.

After the coroner's report was given, a grand jury in the court of Justice Watson M. Rogers handed down four indictments on May 15th that charged Mary and James with the first-degree murder of Sarah Brennan. Both were found guilty and sent to Auburn for execution in the electric chair. Mary's date with the chair was March 29, 1909. Several appeals were made on her behalf, and all were unsuccessful. Hughes, the governor of New York state declared that the sentence of the court will stand. On the day before her execution, she wrote a letter to Reverend J.J. Hickey which exonerated James.

My husband, James D. Farmer, never had any hand in Sarah Brennan's death nor never knew anything about it until the trunk was opened. I never told him anything what had happened. I feel he has been terribly wronged. James D. Farmer was not at home the day the affair happened, neither did James D. Farmer ever put a hand on Sarah Brennan after her death. Again, I wish to say as strongly as I can that my husband, James D. Farmer, is entirely innocent of the death of Sarah Brennan, that he knowingly had no part in any plans that lead to it and that he knew nothing whatever about it. Signed - Mary Farmer.

James was released from prison and plans remained in place to execute Mary. At 6 am on March 29, 1909, Mary was strapped in the electric chair. Her last words were a prayer for her soul - *"Jesus, Mary and Joseph, have mercy on me."* At 6:05, the current was turned on and ten minutes later she was pronounced dead. Mary Farmer was the second woman in the state to die in the electric chair.

Booked the Gravesend Bus

BYE, BYE BABY

Sometime before August 1910, 19-year-old Jennie Perrin began a relationship with Bert Thompson, a former National Guardsman, who was married to his second wife. Jennie became pregnant with Bert's baby which, if discovered, could become very troublesome for him. Bert and her parents were the only people who knew about her condition, and she had told them just two months before her death.

Around 8pm on January 21, 1911, Jennie told her parents she was going "downtown," according to one account to get bananas, and left their Culver Avenue home. About an hour later she came home and went to her room to lie down. Soon she began to scream, moan and writhe in pain. Jennie's father rushed to his daughter's side. Between the waves of pain, he learned from Jennie that Bert had taken her to "Pearl's doctor" on Child Street, where she was given some "medicine" that she took. He then asked her who was responsible for her current condition, Jennie responded "Bert Thompson, and no one else."

A doctor was called to the Perrin home, but Jennie died before he arrived, and most importantly before she could reveal the name of the mysterious doctor. It was a young life snuffed out too soon.

This was a classic murderous story of adultery. When one of the parties is taken out of the picture, it is easy for the other to deny having been involved or even having known the deceased. Bert denied that he knew Jennie, however that lie was exposed. During the coroner's inquest, evidence was presented that contradicted his testimony. A postcard addressed to Jennie while he was stationed at Farnham, Maine as well as a photo of Bert that was found in her trunk. The explanation given by Bert about the discoveries was that she must have stolen these items from an acquaintance. Apparently, he was romantic with more than one Jennie. Hmmmm.

As for knowing her, Jennie's parents and even Bert, at one time, admitted having been a guest in the Perrin home on several occasions.

Bert claimed to have an alibi for the night of Jennie's death. He said that he wasn't with her, in fact he said that he hadn't spoken to her for eight months. He testified that he was at a wrestling match at the State Armory to see Ackerman vs. Albright for the welterweight championship. It was a good alibi; however, no one could corroborate his attendance because he knew no one there. So, was he really at the armory? Or did he carry out a sinister plot to rid himself of Jennie and all the problems their baby would bring for him.

The determination from the autopsy was that Jennie died from (according to her death certificate) was convulsions and pus in the kidneys with her pregnancy as a contributing factor. Jennie had told her father that the mysterious doctor gave her some sort of medicine. What could it have been? She was in and out of convulsions before she died. The kidney condition which her death does not have convulsions as a symptom. I believe that Jennie was poisoned, possibly by strychnine, which causes convulsions and death within 60-90 minutes when administered in the proper does. What do you think?

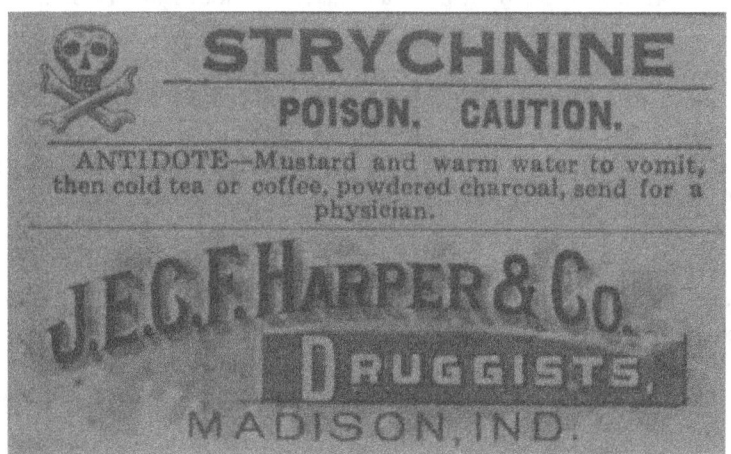

DEATH (AND DINNER) IN THE FROZEN NORTH

Frederick Kislingbury was the first Arctic explorer from Rochester, in fact he was the only Arctic explorer from Rochester. The story of his demise may have given anyone second thoughts about traveling to the north pole. Kislingbury was part of Adolphus Greely's Lady Franklin Bay expedition (July 1881 – July 1884). It was a scientific mission to set up a meteorological station as well as to collect magnetic and astrological data.

On August 11, 1881, the Proteus dropped twenty-five men and supplies off at Lady Franklin Bay on Ellesmere Island, 1,100 miles above the Arctic Circle. The ship would return the following August to resupply the camp. The summer of 1881 was unseasonably warm, which lulled the crew of the Proteus and the members of the expedition into a false sense of security, but winter came with a vengeance.

When the supply tried to reach Lady Franklin Bay in 1882, ice and severe weather stopped them which caused them to turn back. For reasons of safety and, of course finances, no further attempts were made and the men at Greely's camp would have to wait another year. It would then be a rescue mission.

The Proteus headed back to the upper reaches of the world again in 1883 and was crushed by the thick ice and sank. (Ruh, roh Shaggy!)

Fortunately. Greely had a plan in place in case supplies did not reach them for two consecutive summers. Greely and his team packed up their camp, boarded small boats and headed south to Cape Sabine, where emergency supplies should have been left. It took them months to reach the cape, and winter began to set in by October. The Neptune never reached to drop off point, so the men, tired and hungry, found that they had only forty-days' worth of supplies waiting for them. They were forced to make a tough decision – to chance the 720-mile journey on the open sea to Greenland, which would most likely lead to certain death or winter on Cape Sabine and pray that they would be able to stretch the meager food stores until summer. It was a long and deadly 9 months.

Four rescue ships were sent by William Chandler, the Secretary of the Navy, in 1884 to bring the expedition home. When the ships reached Greely's men at the cape on June 22nd, only seven men were still alive...barely.

What John Colwell witnessed when he came ashore can only be conveyed in his own words. "I crawled in (the tent) and took him by the hand, saying to him, 'Greely, is this you?' 'Yes,' said Greely in a faint broken voice, hesitating and shuffling with his words, 'Yes – seven us are left – here we are – dying – like me. Did what I came to do – beat the best record.' Then he fell back exhausted."

The eighteen men died from starvation, hypothermia, or drowning, with a few exceptions. One man by the name of Private Henry was shot for stealing food from their meager supply. It is noted that Frederick Kislingbury died on June 1, 1884, just three weeks before the rescue ships arrived. The cause of his death was allegedly from injuries sustained from a fall off an iceberg. With only forty days of food, how did the survivors make it 264 days? Rumors of cannibalism were vehemently denied by Greely and the others. Though it was written in Sergeant David Brainard's journal that "this growing hunger has driven from our minds all other thoughts and feelings; and like animals, we have little left except for the instinct of eating."

The remains of the deceased, along with the survivors, were loaded onto the ships for the long journey home. The families of the dead expeditioners, including Kislingbury's, were given instructions not to open the caskets of their loved ones. At the time no one knew what was hiding from them. Frederick's brother was happy to hear that his brother died because of an accident and not hunted down like an animal. But he could not ignore the rumors and felt that he needed to know the truth. An autopsy of Kislingbury's body was conducted in the 1865 chapel at Mount Hope cemetery after it was exhumed from its burial plot, which revealed a different story than they had been told. The August 15, 1884, edition of the Democrat and Chronicle reported the grisly findings in great detail.

"We found the body in an iron casket. On the lid being removed it was taken from the casket and placed upon a table. It was packed in cotton batting and encased with cotton cloth tied with string.

Removing this it was found wrapped in a woolen blanket the whole length. Removing this the body was in view. Its weight approximated in our opinion about fifty pounds. On examination of the head, no signs of wounds or injuries were visible. The skin was not broken. The ears and nose were intact. The eyes were sunken and wasted. The hair was thick, and from five to six inches long. The face was covered with a heavy reddish beard and moustache. One the right side of the upper jaw there were seven teeth, the last molar being gone. One the left side three teeth were gone, one incisor and two molars. On the lower jaw two teeth, molars, were gone. The skin and muscles on the anterior portion of the face and neck were intact. From the upper portion of the sternum and clavicle to the border of the fifth rib on the left side, the skin and muscles have all been removed down to the ribs. On the right side, the skin, and muscles down to the lower border of the last rib were gone. There were two openings between the fourth and fifth intercostal spaces into the thoracic cavity. The skin and muscles on the anterior portion of the abdomen intact to the crest of ilium or pelvic bones. Genital organs intact. Muscles and skin of the anterior and posterior portion of the thighs were entirely removed, except the skin on the anterior portion of the knee joints. Muscle and skin of the left leg removed within three inches of the ankle joint. On the right left skin and muscles removed within five inches of the ankle joint. Both feet were intact, toes all present. There was no vestige of integument or muscle on either arm, including the muscles of shoulder blades to wrist joints, except on the right forearm, the interosseous membrane remaining. Flesh and muscles on both hands intact. Examination of the posterior portion of the body showed that the skin and muscles of the back from the seventh cervical vertebrae to the sacrum had been dissected or cut completely away down to the bones, with the exception of pieces of skin from two to three inches square on each side of the upper portion of the sacrum. The pelvic bones were completely denuded. All the extremities were attached to the body by ligaments only. No fractures of the bones of the body were discovered. We found all the organs of the thorax and abdomen present. There was evidence of recent inflammation of the stomach and bowels. The large intestine was distended with hardened lumps of fecal matter, in which there was hair, moss and woody fiber.

In our opinion, the flesh removed was cut away with some sharp instrument. That remaining on the feet, hands and face showed no sign of decomposition. - Charles Buckley, MD and FA Mandeville, MD"

Frederick Kislingbury's brother released a statement, in which he said *"I was told that the remains were all right, but much decomposed. They said I ought not to examine them but should try and remember him as he was in life...They wanted to cover up their guilt. They knew that a portion of the remains have been eaten and - well, they deceived us, but we have found out that condition, and it is probable that every one of the bodies will be disinterred."*

According to Dr. Geoffrey Clark, a doctor who spent twenty years researching Greely's expedition, six bodies belonging to the deceased were stripped of their flesh and four corpses were missing. Aside from Kislingbury's family, one other family opened the coffin to find that the remains had been cannibalized. In 1884 and again in 2015, the family of Private Henry petitioned the courts to allow his body to be exhumed and examined to finally put to rest their questions about what happened to him postmortem. At this time, I cannot find any results of a forensic autopsy.

The ghastly picked bones of the dead officer speak volumes of history.

Frederick Kislingbury

SHARP KNIFE OF A SHORT LIFE

Someone heard screams and the "patter of feet" coming from inside Winnie Burlingame's Stephens Street home. Mrs. Baker knocked on the front door to check on her, but she did not answer. She turned the doorknob, which was unopened, and Mrs. Baker let herself in. What she found on the other side was not what she expected or wanted to see again. Widow Burlingame was lying on her parlor floor in a pool of blood.

The original December 8, 1934 newspaper article about Mrs. Burlingame's death painted a vivid picture of the scene. "...*Down and up the stair the blood stains continued. About eight feet from the foot of the stairs was a big pool of blood. In this was found the woman's dental plates broken to bits. Directly beneath the vice in the cellar bottom was a blood-stained hatchet with hair adhering. The bloody trail led upstairs in the bathroom at the head of the stairs on the ground floor, into the kitchen, dining room and thence into the parlor. The popular theory seems to be that the woman was murdered in the cellar of the home and left supposedly dead; that the killer fled and the woman crawled up the stairs and groped around the rooms until overtaken by death in the parlor...*" The police investigators provided the reporters with some powerful quotes. The victim had "25 gashes in her skull apparently made by a hatchet or knife." She was "virtually scalped by the killer, who apparently attempted to burn the body after the crime," that "acid burns were found on her clothing and her underskirt was seared by flames in several places." There was a "bloody piece of pipe" at the scene. And the boldest statement of all was that Mrs. Burlingame "was murdered after a struggle."

When the police arrived, they found Mrs. Burlingame's head and face bloodied. There was half a bottle of carbolic acid on the floor next to her body and acid burns on her clothing. There was some bruising on her throat. And a trail of blood went throughout the house from the second floor to the cellar, where they found a bloody hatchet on the floor. What wasn't found added to their suspicion of homicide. There was no evidence of carbolic acid or poison in her organs, blood or on the dead woman's hands. The bloody fingerprints had appeared to have been wiped from the handle of the hatchet, for the amount of blood shed, it was oddly clean.

There was no evidence of robbery, $330 in cash and a $50 government bond had not been taken. But when the police talked to the family, the daughter-in-law told them about a strange conversation that had taken place not long before her death. Mrs. Burlingame said that "if anything happens to me, look in the secret pocket of my corset." Lo and behold, the pocket was unbuttoned and empty. What was in her corset that was so valuable that she would protect it with her life?

Even though the crime scene screamed murder the December 8th article offered this confusing statement – "Coroner GL Whiting said he 'leans towards the suicide' theory, but office Clarence Fredericks of the Canisteo police, investigating the death, said he thought that a murderer lay in wait in the cellar of the woman's home." Two days later, the police received a letter alluding to the fact that Winnie was murdered. The anonymous letter started with "You are on the right track."

What made the coroner suspect Winnie Burlingame had taken her own life? Three things. First, even with all the blows to her head and face, her skull was not fractured. He believed that the bruises on her neck were from Mrs. Burlingame's failed attempt to cut her jugular with the hatchet. And two of her sons said she had been worried and depressed about business affairs, lost a considerable amount of money and had a recent business foreclosure. Though, at the time of her death, she owned one of the largest business blocks in Canisteo.

After reviewing the reports of Albert and Robert Hamilton, who were professional criminologists out of Buffalo, it was determined that Winnie Burlingame, so distraught by her lot in life, took her own life with a series of hatchet blows to the head. And even though she had only moved into the house a week before her death and was friendly with the neighbors she was labeled as a depressed recluse.

All this does not take into account that ten days after Mrs. Burlingame's death and just twelve miles away, Lydia Beekman-Parker, also a wealthy widow, died in a similar way – her head was bashed in with no sign of a robbery. A December 19, 1934 Star-Gazette article headlined with *"The murder of Mrs. Lydia Beekman-Parker of Bath and the death of Mrs. Winnie Burlingame of Canisteo are parallel in many respects but not connected, Steuben County authorities state."* A mentally ill mad confessed to Mrs. Beekman-Parker's death. Some say that he was coerced in his statements but was not even questioned about Mrs. Burlingame.

My final thoughts are:

I find it absurd that anyone believes that someone would be so committed to taking their own life that they would repeatedly strike themselves in the face and head with a hatchet almost thirty times. As well as wiping down the handle of the hatchet, placing it on the cellar floor before laying on the parlor floor to die, but only after running around the house to leave a bloody trail. In 1934, the top three methods used to commit suicide were by firearm, poisoning or hanging. And women historically chose a quick method, usually by poison or overdose, shying away from a violent death. It does not seem to be a plausible theory.

So, Mrs. Winnie Burlingame was sent into her afterlife labeled as a depressed recluse who committed suicide to end her mortal pain. May you find peace for your soul.

SLEEP WITH THE FISHES

Homer J. Harrison served as a cannoneer with the US Army during World War I. After his discharge he joined the New York State Troopers at Batavia in 1921, He later became commander of the Castile area in Wyoming County. Harrison had a promising career ahead of him, but he would never see his future. On June 19, 1933, he and his son Robert died in a freak fishing accident.

Later in the afternoon Sergeant Harrison took his two sons, Robert and Roger along with fellow trooper HW Beach fishing in a small rowboat on Silver Lake that he rented from Freehauf's boat livery. The fish were calling them, so they rowed about 800 feet offshore and let the anchor out. When they were ready to put their lines in the water, it was discovered that the tackled box was left on shore. The anchor was raised, and Harrison rowed the boat back to retrieve it. It was minor hiccup on the fishing trip, but they were soon back out on the water. The chain of events that followed ended in the death of Homer and Robert Harrison.

When the group returned to the water, they were out further than before. When the anchor was dropped from the boat, according to Beach's story, the that rope attached it to the boat tightened and the boat capsized. Harrison, Beach, and Roger could all swim, but Robert couldn't and struggled to keep his head above water. Beach and Roger made their way to the overturned hull and within an instant Beach said Homer and Robert slipped below the surface.

Boats in the area came to their aid and began to drag the lake. An hour after the incident the lifeless body of Robert was found, almost an hour later Homer Harrison was found. His watch had stopped at 6:10, the hour they went in the water.

There were two anchors on the boat. Homer dropped the first one and Roger was trying to drop the second when, according to authorities he said, "Something slipped and the boat tipped over," Everyone was dumped into the water, but only two resurfaced. After the bodies of Homer and Robert Harrison were recovered, they were taken to the coroner's office for examination and an official ruling on the causes of death. They were thought to be cut and dry cases of drowning. Robert's lungs were filled with water, a classic indication of being drowned. Homer, on the other hand, had no water in his lungs. Even though he had an injury to his forehead from striking it on the side of the boat, it was determined that it was not severe enough to kill him. Surely a mystery even though his death certificate noted drowning.

Was the death of Harrison an accident or could it have been murder? This is a case that I will be digging deeper into.

Homer and Robert Harrison grave

THE DISAPPEARANCE OF WILLIAM MORGAN

William Morgan was born August 7, 1774 in Culpepper, Virginia and is speculated to have died in 1826 somewhere between Canandaigua and Youngstown. The story of his death reminds me of Jimmy Hoffa in the 1970s.

1821 Morgan moved to Upper Canada to open a brewery, which burned down. The financial strains after the fire drove him to return to the United States, where he arrived first in Rochester, New York. While in Rochester he joined a local Mason lodge. He claimed that while he lived in Canada, he became a Master Mason, which is the equivalent of 3rd degree. Now in 1825 he joined the Western Star chapter in Leroy. At that time, he swore to the lodge and its members, on the Bible, that he had acquired the six degrees required to reached Royal Arch status.

In Batavia he attempted to join the lodges there, but the memberships were suspicious of him. They questioned his character and masonic pedigree and denied his admittance. Morgan was a bricklayer and stone cutter, as for his character – it was said that he gambled and drank heavily, though those close to him disputed the claims.

It was after being "blackballed" from membership that Morgan declared that he was going to write a book that exposed all their secrets. Was that his intent all along? To infiltrate the secret society and expose it to the world?

A local newspaper publisher named David Cade Miller gave Morgan a generous advance for the book. Why? Miller began the process of becoming a Mason only to be blackballed by the membership after reaching the level of 1st degree. Morgan agreed to give ¼ of the profits to a group of financial backers in return for $500,000 when the book was ready for publication. In 2024 money, it is equivalent to $15.5 million.

Whether or not Morgan held the level degrees he claimed to hold is unknown and for the remainder of his story irrelevant. The issue is that at some point he placed his hand on the Bible and swore an oath to never reveal the secret rituals, meetings and ceremonies. As with any oath taken on the Bible, breaking it would have dire consequences. Morgan was called out in the newspapers by members of the lodge to condemn and discredit Morgan for his betrayal of the brotherhood of the Masons.

Karma, or most likely the ever-reaching arm of the secret society, repaid Morgan for his misdeeds. The endgame was to keep Morgan from writing "Illustrations of Masonry" and to secure centuries worth of secrets. On September 11, 1826, he was arrested for defaulting on a loan and theft of a shirt and tie. Morgan was sent to jail in Canandaigua, 50 miles to the east. The campaign against him at home was working and Morgan had just a few friends left. David Miller travelled to Canandaigua to bail him out. Freedom was short lived, and he was arrested again, this time he was accused of skipping out on a $2 tavern tab. His sudden and constant trouble with the law seemed to some that Morgan was being set up. What happened next cements that idea. He was taken back to Canandaigua. This time Miller didn't bail him out, a group of men showed up at the jail when the jailer was not there and persuaded his wife to release Morgan to them. She watched William Morgan get into a carriage with the men and that was the last time he was seen alive.

MORGAN PLACED IN THE MAGAZINE OF OLD FORT NIAGARA.

One of the rumors as to what happened to Morgan was after leaving the jail, he was taken to Niagara County, loaded onto a boat and dumped into Lake Ontario with a stone tied to his feet a mile from shore. Whether that was how it played out, no one knows for sure. More than a year after his disappearance, a body washed up on shore in such a condition that it was hard to make a positive identification. Many believed that it was the waterlogged and decomposed body of William Morgan. The body was originally buried as Morgan, but a Canadian woman claimed that the clothing the body was wearing belonged to her husband, Timothy Monroe. So, the mystery remained unsolved.

Even though Morgan's body was not positively identified, charges in connection with his disappearance were filed. Eli Bruce, Mason and Niagara County sheriff served 28 months for his role in Morgan's kidnapping. 3 men – Leton Lawson, Nicholas Cheseboro and Edward Sawyer, were also convicted for kidnapping Morgan. Because no one knows whether he was exiled to Canada or was in fact murdered, no charged were ever filed in connection with his death.

There is a ghost story associated with William Morgan along the shores of Lake Ontario. It is said that the stone tied to Morgan's feet somehow came to be in Shubal Merritt's possession. He kept is as a centerpiece in his garden at what is now Marjim Manor in Somerset. Shubal's son Lewis used to move the stone around the property and Morgan's ghost would haunt the grounds looking for it. After Lewis was accidentally shot by Shubal, Morgan's ghost seemed to move on.

Breathed One's Last

SOMETHING IN THE WATER

The wheels of fate for North Boston, New York were set into motion when Ephraim Tuel Merrifield left his Warwick, Massachusetts home in September 1843. Merrifield embarked on an adventure to the western frontier at a time when New England was in the grip of a typhoid fever epidemic. When he left home on his journey, Merrifield felt fine, never better. But as the days passed, he began to feel ill and needed a rest. He stopped at Fuller's Tavern in North Boston, a small Erie County village with a population of only 43 people.

Merrifield had diarrhea, a fever and other symptoms that would eventually be identified as the classic signs of typhoid fever. On October 9th, 28 days after he arrived in village, the 21-year-old died. And in those brief four weeks, Ephraim Merrifield left a horrible mark on the community. In little less than two months, 28 of the 43 residents became violently and mysteriously, and ten of them died.

At the time it was not fully understood how the fever spread. Dr. Austin Flint, a doctor from Buffalo, found that each of the patients had one thing in common; they all drew water from the well at Fuller's Tavern. How did the sickness get into the well? The outhouse of the tavern was very close to the well and the disease that came from Merrifield's bowels seeped into the ground water which fed the well.

Interestingly, it was originally thought that the Stern family contaminated the well in retaliation after a fight with the tavern owner resulted in the Sterns being banned from using the tavern's well because they were the only family not touched by the illness. The belief was that Mr. Stern had dumped some kind of chemical into the water. But through Dr. Flint's research the Stern family was cleared of any malicious wrongdoing.

The Fuller Tavern was torn down in 1973 after being deemed structurally unsafe.

YOU GIVE ME FEVER

Genesee Fever was a deadly epidemic from 1790-1812 that spread throughout the "Genesee Country," or Western New York. The fever was a conglomeration of malaria, typhus and typhoid fever, mainly caused by living close to swampy, wet areas along the Genesee River. The region had a reputation of being "one of the least healthy areas of the state."

The hardest hit were the settlers at King's Landing, also known as Hansford Landing, near present-day Kodak Park. Gideon King and Colonel Zadock Granger founded King's Landing, along with six families who moved there in the fall 1797. Gideon's was the first in the settlement to succumb to the disease in 1798. The King's Landing Cemetery was established to hold his remains, over which his wife erected a stone that reads – "The Genesee Fever was mortal to most heads of the families in 1798 and prevented further settlements till about 1815." Also in 1798, Gideon's sons Daniel and Bildad as well as his brother-in-law Daniel Graham died. It is believed that in 1798 alone 20 people at King's Landing lost the battle with Genesee Fever. A year later Zadock Granger was dead, along with more of the settlers. By 1800 Thomas King and Eli Granger were the only two settlers from the original six families that survived the fever.

One of the earliest cases of multiple death due to the Genesee Fever took place on Samuel Street's farm in Scottsville along Dugan's Creek. What happened at the farm in 1790 is looked at through the eyes of Jeremiah Olmstead, his brother-in-law and current resident at King's Landing Cemetery. Shortly after Jeremiah and his wife Rachel settled on the farm, the disease took hold and killed 10 members of the Street family and farm hands. Jeremiah and Rachel were spared, but he would lose her 5 years later.

More than three decades later, a different fever gripped the area – Lake Fever, which ran along the northern and southern shores of Lake Ontario. This fever was cholera and in less than two months it took the lives of 121 Rochesterians in 1832. 168 years later, Tragically Hip recorded a song about it aptly titled Lake Fever.

Death by Misadventure

HE BURNED THEM UP

The Steuben County poorhouse in the 1870s housed an average of 125 of the county's poorest and most vulnerable citizens and offered them basic care to support a very meager existence. Besides paupers, they also had individuals who were insane, epileptic, elderly, disabled and mentally handicapped. According to an annual report, *"only one-third could be trusted to take care of themselves."* The buildings at the county facility were overcrowded and understaffed, and what staff there was undertrained. This led to the tragic loss of life in the early morning hours of April 8, 1878.

New York State had passed the Willard Asylum Act of 1865, which mandated all people diagnosed insane to be put in state asylums to protect those in the county homes as well as provide them with more adequate care. The Children's Act was adopted into law in 1875 to remove all children 3-16 from poorhouses and place them in orphan asylums for their protection. But often small county homes either did not have the funds to move those "inmates" to the proper facilities or thought they knew best what their neighbors needed and shirked the law, which also played a major role in the morning's tragic events.

"Only Paupers," the Princeton Union headline read on page two of the April 17, 1878 edition of their paper.

April 7, 1878 was a normal day at the poorhouse. Right on schedule at 9 p.m. the doors of the inmates' room and the doors of the building were locked from the outside; they said for both the safety of the inmates and that of the community. Little did they know that a human powder keg was about to explode.

L.C. Ford, who was from Hornellsville, was an "inmate" at the home. He was there because he suffered from epileptic seizures and was also insane – considered to be violent and dangerous to himself and others. In fact, L.C. Ford's mental state was recorded in July 1876 after an examination by Dr. John L. Selover who told Mr. Carrington (the caretaker) and the superintendent that Ford was too insane to be housed at the poorhouse. Furthermore, he believed that Ford was capable of killing someone or setting a fire to *"burn them up if he was not cared for."* L.C. had not had an "episode" in a while and had been "suspiciously quiet" (my words, not theirs) lately. Now as a parent, you become suspicious when your rambunctious and loud child is too quiet, because their quietness usually means they are getting into mischief. In the situation regarding the poorhouse, they thought Ford's quietness was a good thing and left him under the supervision of his roommate – a man who was physically disabled and blind. Not a good decision on their part. During the night L.C. set fire to his room, which quickly spread through the two-story building.

According to a January 1879 annual report, *"Ford was greatly excited up to nearly the time of the fire. He had torn his bed in pieces and scattered the straw about the floor."* Ford then set the straw on fire with a match. Ford stuck his head through the bars of his window screaming "Murder!" His head became stuck. Within minutes flames came out of the window and enveloped his head, killing him. Although smoke filled the building, the flames were contained to Ford's room until the door was opened by his roommate.

Let's back up for a moment before continuing with more details of the horrible fire. How did L.C. Ford, a dangerous insane man who the doctor predicted would "burn them up," get a match. The superintendents of the county poorhouse gave the "inmates" (oh how I hate that word) tobacco, pipes and matches to smoke during the day – even L.C. Ford. And no one searched Ford for matches before he was locked in for the night.

Who had the keys to the building? No one knows. The superintendent was not onsite, most likely at home or the home of someone else doing who knows what. Eli Carrington, who was the caretaker, and another employee at the home forced their way into the building, saving as many as they could before being driven back by the flames. Staff and "inmates" from the other buildings battled the fire as well, with no fire equipment and little water to extinguish it. In one case, a patient with one leg and crutch for support broke a window to pull a mother and child to safety. Another door was broken down and nearly a dozen people staggered out of the heavy smoke.

Where was the fire department? An account from Minnesota paper reported – *"The county home is about two miles from Bath*

Court House Bridge. *The light was noticed in Bath just before 1 o'clock a.m. It did not appear like a fire in the distance, and at first nothing was done, but the nature of the glare of light finally became apparent, and the Bath fire department was called out by the alarm...their services were all unavailing, either to succor the burning inmates or save the building..."* Within half an hour the roof fell in and all anyone could do was watch the orange glow of the flames until it burned out. The fire burned so hot that little was left of the sixteen who perished. What remained *"was in a horrible mass of ashes, human bones, iron, windows, grating, bed-steads and debris. It will be impossible to recover any of the bodies in a recognizable form. The ashes of the whole fifteen lie buried in the ruins of the burned building."*

The youngest of the victims – Jennie Mills aged four years and Mary Hewitt just fourteen months – were under the charge of two women at the home who had children of their own. It was an ideal arrangement to have a motherly figure of the girls – that is until the fire started. Both women abandoned Jennie and Mary, escaping with their children and leaving the girls to perish in the flames.

As with all deaths in the late 1800s, there was a coroner's inquest to place blame on the deadly event. According to the coroner's verdict, these two statements stand out. *"...for not persisting in the removal of L.C. Ford, after receiving information that he was not a proper person to remain at the poorhouse..."* and *"...by our superintendents promptly moving all such persons as L.C. Ford, and placing an outside flight of stairs as a means of egress from the building used for sleeping rooms, such a calamity as we just had may be averted."*

The most important revelation made about the sixteen deaths was that they *"came to their deaths through the gross negligence of the board of supervisors in not providing suitable buildings for the accommodations and protection of the paupers kept at the county poor-house, and I find the board of supervisors, and each member of that board, guilty of manslaughter in the fourth degree."*

The newspaper headline said, "Only Paupers."

LIGHTNING STRIKES BUT ONCE

A storm brewed and dark clouds passed in front of the sun on the afternoon of July 15, 1890. Before a single drop of rain could fall something terrible happened in Conesus. George McKeown was "cocking up" hay with a pitchfork as the sky grew angry. At the same time the pitchfork was raised above his head, a bolt of lightning cracked through the air, stuck the tines, and burned a mark on the wooden handle before entering the boy's body. He was killed instantly.

Stay away from windows during a thunderstorm. I used to believe that that was just on an old wives' tale, however there is some merit to this warning. The July 13, 1897 edition of the Rochester Democrat and Chronicle reported that a resident of Geneva in Ontario County was killed by lightning while closing a window during a storm. The readers were also advised to stay away from chimneys and stoves.

On August 17, 1898, a line of dangerous thunderstorms passed over Western New York and left a path of death and destruction. A telegraph operator named Jarvis was rendered unconscious when the electrical shock from a nearby lightning strike travelled through the wires into his telegraph machine while he sat at in the office at the Northern Central Station in Newark. 35-year-old W. Henry Slater from Lancton's Corners near Elba was killed instantly while standing in his woodshed. I bolt of lightning blew apart the shed, turning it into splinters before entering his chest. On the same fateful day, 3 horses in Oakfield were killed during the electrical storm while Henry Blodgett and his team were plowing a field. Blodgett was knocked unconscious but recovered.

MOURN THE LITTLE CHILDREN

1911 was a tragic year from the Murphy family of Maple Street in Gates. Charles was only 11 years old when he died on June 11th. Charles, his brother Francis and George Harrington, their neighbor, were just doing what boys do...exploring the suburban jungle surrounding their homes. Standing at the entrance of a freshly dug canal tunnel on Buffalo Road, the imagination of any boy would be jump-started and the urge to explore it would almost be inescapable. The dangling array of wires mimicked the vines of an ancient forest or the vipers in a wild jungle. Harrington ducked under the wires as he entered the tunnel, but Charles instinctively reached up to move them from his path and grabbed hold of a live wire and was killed instantly by 4,100 volts.

A coroner's inquest was called on 15th of June. The gentleman in charge of the project testified that there were "no trespassing signs" posted at the excavation site. But it was determined that a different approach should have been taken. *"It was shown that it would have been easy to unhook the conveyor feed wires from the general trolley feed wire and that then there would have been no danger."*

Subsequently, a July 1, 1911, newspaper article announced that the superintendent was deemed negligent in the death of Charles Murphy. Not only could the power have been disconnected from the wires, but a grab machine used to take up the wire slack had allowed the wire to sag 3' 10" above the ground. As well as the insulation on the wire was worn exactly where Charles had grabbed it, giving him the entire 4,100 volts.

This, unfortunately, was not the only tragedy that fell on the Murphy family that year. 6 months later, on December 19th Charles's 10-year-old sister Isabelle passed away at St. Mary's Hospital from an illness.

Both children lay at rest at Holy Sepulchre Cemetery in Rochester.

PL~~AN~~ES, TRAINS AND AUTOMOBILES

We mindlessly cross railroad tracks every day, relying on the flashing lights and gates to warn us of an oncoming train. But it took thousands of fatal train vs. car accidents to prompt its invention and implementation. A 43-day span in late Spring 1922 proved deadly in Genesee County, leaving 10 dead and almost 75 injured.

65-year-old Thomas R Brodie, a local farmer, was traveling on Lake Street in North Le Roy that Saturday morning, May 13, 1922. He stopped his Buick sedan at the crossing before proceeding across the tracks. How Thomas did not see the train coming, no one knows. Witnesses reported that they thought they saw him look both ways. The Lehigh Valley Black Diamond Express was barreling at speeds of 65-70 miles per hour before it broadsided the sedan. The impact caused Thomas to be thrown from his car, killing him instantly. The car was wedged under the front of the train engine with sparks flying as it was pushed 300 yards down the track. This caused the train to derail and send the coaches over a 40-foot embankment. EE Croser, a yardman was crushed by the smoking car was killed as was a travelling salesman named LE Clay. Mrs. Russell Burchfield and Mrs. Arthur Deroire were seriously injured and died at the hospital the following day. An investigation was launched to determine the cause of the crash. The verdict exonerated the engineer stating that Mr. Thomas Brodie misjudged how fast the train was going when he crossed the tracks.

4 days later and a few miles down the track, tragedy struck again. Fred Schrienier, a heavy truck driver, had just picked up 8 tons of stone from the Le Roy Lime and Crushed Stone Quarry that was to be delivered to a construction crew working on the Batavia-Byron Road. As he crossed the tracks at the plant, his truck was hit by a Buffalo, Rochester & Pittsburgh Railroad passenger train. Fred was killed instantly. As weird as it may sound, the train could not have hit the truck more perfectly. Had it struck a few feet back, the

truck would have overturned and spilled 8 tons of crushed stone onto the train and caused a major and fatal derailment.

The last accident happened on June 25, 1922, in Corfu near the train station. George Perrin, VP of the Bank of Genesee in Batavia, and his family decided to take a drive to Buffalo after church that afternoon. On the way home, George Jr. was driving while mom and grandmother, Mrs. Theodore Burch, sat in the back seat. As they entered a "snipe" grade or level crossing, the New York Central No. 3 headed for Chicago struck the car. Mr. and Mrs. Perrin were killed instantly. Mrs. Burch died within minutes and George Jr. died at the hospital in Batavia less than two hours later. In just moments an entire family was wiped out.

STEAM GAUGE AND LAMP WORKS FIRE

Around 7:30 in the evening on November 9, 1888, while 250 men were at work in the Steam Gauge and Lantern Works factory, flames erupted in the building along the Genesee River gorge. The fire was first discovered by Jacob Diehl, the night watchman, and a call came from fire box no. 91 near the Rochester Cotton Factory on Center Street. The fire was so intense that just five minutes after the first alarm came, a second alarm sounded.

Fire chief Bemish quickly assessed the situation and when he got to the northside of the building, along the rocky edge of the river gorge, he saw the body of a dying man who had jumped. Bemish then looked up at the panicked faces of the factory workers on the third and fourth floors. They pleaded for help. He ordered his men to grab the net and position it between the building and the gorge. The November 10, 1888 edition of the Rochester Democrat and Chronicle had this to say about the rescue of those men – *"The men in the burning building were from thirty to forty feet above the ledge, and down they came fast. Not a few landed in the net and their fall was thus broken. So frantic were they however that frequently a man jumped too far away, striking the rocks with a sound which made those who heard it shudder with horror. In ten minutes all who could be seen on the northside had struck the net or the ground."*

While rescues were attempted on the north and south sides, crews battled the flames from the east and west but were hindered with accessibility. The heavy wood beams and planking fueled the inferno. Some say that the fire started in the basement and used the elevator shaft as an oxygen source, allowing the flames to shoot up through it and trap workers on the upper floors. Firefighters knew the building could not be saved once the flames burst through the roof. At that point, all they could do was protect the buildings around the factory. Within thirty minutes, the Steam Gauge and Lantern Works building was gutted.

The headline in the November 10th edition of The Evening World out of New York City read – *"Twenty Lives Lost at Rochester, Only One Fire Escape, So the Men Jumped as Sam Patch Did."* The article painted a short and grim scene of events. *"No fewer then twenty lives were lost and over twenty persons injured by last night's fire at the Steam Gauge and Lantern Company's works. The damage us at least $250,000. When the firemen arrived the windows on the street side of the building were filled with men calling for help. There were sixty-five men inside. The firemen cautioned them not to jump; that they would soon be rescued. To this the men paid no attention and soon the air was filled with falling human bodies. Thirty men jumped from the third story, all of whom were more or less injured. They were at once taken to hospitals. Four of them died of injuries before they could be removed. There are twenty-one men missing, all of whom it is supposed are dead and in the ruins. The building is on the verge of the upper falls of the Genesee, where Sam Patch jumped to his death years ago."*

Ruins of the Steam Lantern building the day after the fire

Witnesses saw horrible and desperate acts of survival which the newspaper somberly relayed to their readers. Two men were seen in a third-floor window just above the falls right after the first alarm sounded. *"They stood for a moment undecided what to do, when suddenly one leaped out and fell in the water about ten feet from the brink of the precipice. He was immediately followed by the other man. One of them apparently recovered himself and was unhurt as he waded through the water until he was under the bridge, where he was rescued by a party of who lowered a ladder to him. As soon as he reached terra-firma he started to run towards State Street and disappeared. No trace of the other man was discovered, and it is presumed he was so badly injured that he could not help himself, and he remained there and was buried under the wall which fell ten minutes later."*

There were many stories of individuals who escaped and who perished. The Democrat and Chronicle was filled with stories of heartbreak and hope. There was the story of the Fox brothers. Amid the smoke and chaos both brothers searched for the other until they came face to face. They rushed to each other in an embrace so joyful it was as if they had been separated forever. Those who witnessed the moment, even the strongest of me, found the need to dry their eyes. Patrolman Youle met the wife of Gall, one of the factory foremen on State Street. She had her little boy which her who said, "Let us go back home; I guess papa's got there by this time." As they walked away, the officer didn't have the heart to tell the little bot that his papa would not be home again.

Firemen at the scene battled the flames and put life and limb on the line to save as many as they could; as did John McCormick. McCormick was a member of Active Hose No. 2 and had been directing the water stream into the fire when something struck him on the hand and caused a bleeding gash. *"...A Democrat and Chronicle reporter who chanced to stand near him drew out his handkerchief and quickly bound it up. Mr. McCormick returned to work after having the injured member attended by a physician. He carried the hose up to the top of the Briggs Building."*

All accounts of the tragedy put the death toll at 34 men, but according to witnesses, at least one woman perished in the flames. Fireman Fogarty saw a girl around 16 inside a third-floor window. The rescue ladder was four feet from the window and before they could reach her, the girl fell back into the heat and smoke of the fire. "Her cries, which were agonizing, were soon stifled." There were no women working in the building at that house and it was ascertained that she must have been there with a workman's lunch.

All but six of the victims' remains were identified. Those six were placed in a single grave at Mt. Hope Cemetery and a memorial to all the victims was erected there in 1898. Inscribed on the memorial is "But God was not in the fire. And after the fire, a still small voice."

Originally the cause of the fire was declared to be arson, an act supposedly committed by John Van Korff, an engineer at the factory. On November 14, 1888, he was arrested and charged but was never tried for arson. The jury in the coroner's inquest found that the fire started in the packing room at the south end of the main building, but exactly how it started is unknown. It was also determined that there was no evidence that John Van Korff had any involvement in the disaster. The December 5, 1888 edition of the Democrat and Chronicle stated that the Honorable W.S. Hubbell believed that *"...nothing further would ever be learned about it unless possibly through some future death-bed confession..."* and that *"...There were other things about this fire, he said, which have been very mysterious in character and about which nothing satisfactory has been learned..."*

136 years later, those mysteries remain unsolved.

THE RACE'S END

Ten autorace fans were killed and 13 seriously injured in Syracuse, NY, when a car driven by Lee Oldfield, brother of Barney Oldfield, blew a tire, lost control, and crashed through a fence at the New York State Fair. – September 16, 1911

The horrific accident happened in the 43rd mile of the 50-mile race. And it was entirely avoidable! Oldfield's car developed trouble with the right front tire. Witnesses reported to have seen it "throw a shoe," which beat the track with each revolution. Oldfield wanted to make a pit stop to have the tire replaced, but he was closing the gap with the De Palma, who was in the lead, and his manager waved him to continue. He showed caution, by slowing down and even cutting his engine when he was in front of the grandstand, but soon he threw that caution to the wind when the lead was in his grasp. Some speculated that De Palma was having car trouble of his own and Oldfield was expecting him to stop, and he could replace his tire then.

As Oldfield rounded the 43rd mile, his nose was at De Palma's rear bumper, and he was ready to make his move. Just then a sound resembling a gunshot came from the track. Moments later Oldfield's car was in the air sailing through the safety fence. It stopped twenty feet into the crowd. People screamed as they scrambled from the path of destruction. According to the New York Times, "*Oldfield was thrown out and was unconscious when help reached him. The car, when its progress was checked, it was turned on its side. One man's body was hurled into the air and landed in the crowd some feet from the place where struck. One boy was decapitated.*"

DePalma was unaware of the tragedy. But I can't imagine that he missed the chaos when he rounded the track the remaining 7 laps. Race officials were aware of what had transpired but refused to call the race. Ironically, after DePalma crossed the finish line one of his rear tires exploded.

DEATH ON THE RAILS

Between Old Forge and Inlet on Route 28, in the Adirondack Mountains, is a sign that reads, "*Train Wreck Here on Nov. 9. 1913 Train struck a log, derailed, and went over the cliff killing 3 of its crew.*"

Storms ripped through the Adirondacks in November 1913 and trees were down all over the area. Horses with chains were used to clear the debris, so clean-up efforts were slow. "Track walkers" were paid to do just that, walk the tracks and report any obstructions, damage, etc. It is unknown why the section of tracks east of Eagle Bay had not been checked, but it had tragic and deadly consequences.

As darkness started to fall in the mountains, the train driven by Engineer Benjamin Hall headed up the Raquette Lake track. Around 5:30 in the evening it struck a fallen tree that was across the track which caused the locomotive and tender to plunge over the embankment, taking Hall, fireman John Case and brakeman A.G. Lashaway to their death.

Conductor John Rank suffered minor injuries and walked six and half miles to the nearest telegraph office in Carter. Help would not be quick to arrive, the storm had taken down power and telegraph lines. The same storm system that ultimately caused the death of these three men was also responsible for other railroad accidents across the northeast and Great Lakes that resulted in nearly three hundred fatalities.

Took the
Last Train
to Glory

INTO THE DARKNESS

One of the most legitimate fears is the fear of death, but even worse was being buried alive. A horrifying death – being suffocated in a box, six feet underground.

Over the centuries, what would become traditions, were put in place to ensure that the deceased in fact dead. "Sitting up with the dead" was in part to guarantee that their dearly departed loved one was on their way to the great beyond. After the body was washed and prepared for burial, family and friends took turns sitting by the body twenty-four hours a day for three days, after which death was certain.

When funeral homes were put in charge of the final preparations, that sense of certainty lessened. To achieve the same peace of mind, devices were invented to save those who may have been prematurely buried. The grave bell was one of them. It consisted of a string in the coffin that was run through a pipe and attached to a bell above ground. If the "deceased" awoke from their slumber, they would simply pull the string to ring the bell and hope someone topside would hear it.

The newspapers reported the stories of those who died once they were set in the ground, for even though it was a fear of most – it made for good reading.

After the burial of Frances Burke from Dunkirk in February 1892, her family had second thoughts as to whether she had been dead or was instead in some sort of trance. By the time the coffin was exhumed, it was filled with water. If Frances had been alive when she was placed in the ground, she surely drowned. Ultimately her death rested on the shoulders of her family because she had been buried without proper examination and permit. And Coroner Blood, aptly named, believed that Frances Burke had been buried alive and drowned.

There were instances where being buried alive came about quite accidentally and without warning. Take the account of James Rearden on March 4, 1887. Rearden worked with a crew of men digging a trench on Adams Street in Rochester for the construction of a municipal sewer system. At the first sign of the north wall of the trench giving way, the men were ordered out. Rearden was hearing impaired and did not notice the danger until it was too late. The wall came crashing down on him, burying him. Frantically, the men worked to free him, but by the time they uncovered his body, he had already expired.

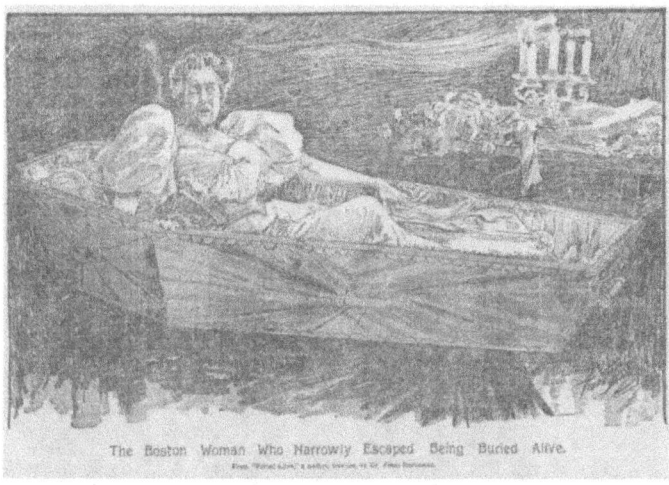

The Boston Woman Who Narrowly Escaped Being Buried Alive.

TAKEN FROM THE GRAVE

Bodies have been snatched from the grave for centuries. Their rest disturbed for more than one reason – the robbery of valuables that were to be carried to the afterlife, revenge, superstition, and the advancement in the medical field. During the mid- to late 1800s, bodies were removed under the dark of night to provide cadavers for medical students to use in their studies. The perpetrators held no discrimination, the dead were equal. Social, economic, and political status offered no protection, all that mattered was the prize the robbers sought just six feet under the freshly mounded earth.

GRAVE-ROBBERS AT WORK.

Mary Buchanan died on February 22, 1862, from consumption, a disease that stole the loves of thousands of young people before they had a chance to live. On March 1st, Mary, just 21 years old, was laid to rest by her grieving family and friends at the Batavia Cemetery on Harvester Avenue. Her mother Rhoda took the tragedy hard, and it did not help that she saw her daughter in her dreams. On three different nights Mrs. Buchanan dreamt the same horrifying scene, her daughter's peace had been broken. These visions caused her distress and to calm herself, she visited Mary's grave. It did not, however, give her the peace of mind that she sought. Mrs. Buchanan found these dreams to be true, Mary's grave was empty. The open coffin only held the remnants of her torn burial clothes.

The alarm was raised and after a short investigation by the sheriff's office, a suspect had been named, and a search of his residence was underway. At the home of Forrest Page, also known as John H. Page, a medical student, parts of the decaying remains of Mary Buchanan were found in a box.

Page was arrested and his trial was set to begin that summer. His indictment read as – *"John H, Page of the town of Elba on the twenty fifth day of February in the year of our Lord one thousand eight hundred and sixty two...with force and arms did enter the public burying ground...did enter the grave there of Mary Buchanan and with force and arms did unlawfully, willfully and indecently did dig, open and carry the body of Mary Buchanan from the grave for the purpose of dissection.* William Bryan served as his defense council and pleaded Page's case under the reasoning that even if he had been illegally in possession of the body of Mary Buchanan, it was done in the name of science and further aid in his education.

At the time of Page's trial, the United States was plunged into a great Civil War. As the number of casualties overwhelmed the military's physicians, students were called to serve. Though Page was ineligible to become a medical cadet due to his criminal trial, he was appointed as an assistant surgeon at Fort Scott in Kansas. With that, he served no prison time for body snatching. Nicknamed "Digging Doctor Page," he died on August 3, 1878, in Buchanan County, Missouri. How ironic.

The easiest victims to target were those at the county poorhouses because they were usually anonymous in both life and death, not to be missed by the living. A man, whose identity had been lost with the passage of time, lived at the Wayne County poorhouse in Lyons. He had an incurable disease which made death come sooner than later. Unlike most inmates at the county home, he had friends who cared for him. Arrangements were made with George Carver, the keeper of the home, to bring his body to Rose when his time came. A letter arrived on January 20, 1881 from Carver informing them of the man's death. Immediately a grave was dug and the next day Henry Garlic, the Rose postmaster and Oscar

Ward, the former town supervisor, left for Lyons to bring their friend home to rest.

When Garlic and Ward arrived at the county home, they were informed that the mail had delayed their notification by ten days. The man's body had been kept as long as it could, but as decomposition began to set in, the decision was made to inter him at the poorhouse cemetery. Intent on keeping their word, Garlic and Ward proceeded to remove the coffin from the fresh grave. They sensed something was not right, it was opened and found to be empty. There were no clues to who could have done such a heinous crime. The man's body was never found.

The cemetery at the Wayne County poorhouse was a frequent haunt for grave robbers. In 1880, a dozen corpses were removed and each year after again that many, more or less. A doctor in Geneva was the recipient of more than one of them. Particularly that of a woman that died at the poorhouse in 1885. Her body was taken ten days after her death and a young farmer earned the modest sum of thirty-eight dollars to deliver it.

In June of 1882, ironically the body-snatcher became the corpse. Dr. Hervey W. Kendall was found shot between the eyes in a meadow near the Onondaga County Poorhouse. By his body was a medical bag filled with tools of the trade – for body snatching.

Students at Syracuse Medical College said that Kendall was a professional resurrectionist. He was bold in his endeavors, not hiding his actions. One time he arrived at the college with a barrel which contained a freshly obtained body. He unloaded it in broad daylight on the front steps of the school.

The night before Kendall's death, he rented a rig from a livery stable with the intent to "get a bod." He was going to see if one might have been recently interred in the poorhouse cemetery, if so, he would dig it up.

At first it was believed that Dr. Kendall had committed suicide, but something did not add up. The wound on his head had a wad of paper inside it, which pointed to his death being murder. The working theory was – a band of vigilantes wanted to stop the man who had defiled the graves in cemeteries across the countryside.

When he was first found, he was still alive – barely. He lingered for nearly a day before all life within him was extinguished. Dr. Hervey W. Kendall was 27 years old.

TELL IT TO THE BEES

Telling the Bees
John Greenleaf Whittier (1858)

Here is the place; right over the hill
Runs the path I took;
You can see the gap in the old wall sill,
And the stepping-stones in the shallow brook.

There is the house, with the gate red-barred,
And the poplars tall;
And the barn's brown length, and the cattle-yard,
And the white horns tossing above the wall.

There are the beehives ranged in the sun;
And down by the brink
Of the brook are her poor flowers, wee-o'errun,
Pansy and daffodil, rose and pink.

Telling the bees is an old tradition where the important events of the beekeeper's life are told to his bees – births, marriages, deaths, etc. It was believed that if the bees were not told or "put into mourning," a penalty was paid, which may include not making honey or leaving the hive for good.

In the 1800's, a piece of wedding cake or a funeral biscuit was given to the bees and the name of the deceased or married couple was told to them.

In New England, the hive was draped with black for mourning, while the spouse or children of the dead hummed a somber tune. Another interesting variation is that the hive would be raised a few inches and when the coffin was lowered into the grave, the hive was lowered back to the ground. In some instances, the hive, draped in black, was positioned to face the funeral procession.

This interesting article appeared in the April 27, 1956 edition of The North Adams Transcript on North Adams, Massachusetts.

Bees Join Mourners at Funeral Today

Throughout his long life, the late John Zepka of 21 Victory Street had raised, worked with and loved bees and was widely known in this section as a man who "had a way with them."

This morning it appeared as though the bees had taken their own way of paying a final tribute to him.

When the funeral cortege reached the grave in St. Stanislaus Cemetery they found the funeral tent literally swarming with bees. They were all over the tent ceiling and clinging to the profuse flower sprays. They made no attempt to annoy the mourners, just remained almost immobile. Persons who saw the spectacle declared that they had never seen anything like it before.

The tradition is still honored today. When Queen Elizabeth II passed away in September 2022, the royal beekeeper told the bees of the monarch's death and Charles III ascension to the throne.

www.ingramcontent.com/pod-product-compliance
Lightning Source LLC
LaVergne TN
LVHW012032060526
838201LV00061B/4567